Editor-in-Chief and Founder:
    Lyndon H. LaRouche, Jr.
Editorial Board: *Lyndon H. LaRouche, Jr. , Helga
    Zepp-LaRouche, Robert Ingraham, Tony
    Papert, Gerald Rose, Dennis Small, Jeffrey
    Steinberg, William Wertz*
Co-Editors: *Robert Ingraham, Tony Papert*
Managing Editor: *Nancy Spannaus*
Technology: *Marsha Freeman*
Books: *Katherine Notley*
Ebooks: *Richard Burden*
Graphics: *Alan Yue*
Photos: *Stuart Lewis*
Circulation Manager: *Stanley Ezrol*

INTELLIGENCE DIRECTORS
Counterintelligence: *Jeffrey Steinberg, Michele
    Steinberg*
Economics: *John Hoefle, Marcia Merry Baker,
    Paul Gallagher*
History: *Anton Chaitkin*
Ibero-America: *Dennis Small*
Russia and Eastern Europe: *Rachel Douglas*
United States: *Debra Freeman*

INTERNATIONAL BUREAUS
Bogotá: *Miriam Redondo*
Berlin: *Rainer Apel*
Copenhagen: *Tom Gillesberg*
Houston: *Harley Schlanger*
Lima: *Sara Madueño*
Melbourne: *Robert Barwick*
Mexico City: *Gerardo Castilleja Chávez*
New Delhi: *Ramtanu Maitra*
Paris: *Christine Bierre*
Stockholm: *Ulf Sandmark*
United Nations, N.Y.C.: *Leni Rubinstein*
Washington, D.C.: *William Jones*
Wiesbaden: *Göran Haglund*

ON THE WEB
e-mail: eirns@larouchepub.com
www.larouchepub.com
www.executiveintelligencereview.com
www.larouchepub.com/eiw
Webmaster: *John Sigerson*
Assistant Webmaster: *George Hollis*
Editor, Arabic-language edition: *Hussein Askary*

EIR (ISSN 0273-6314) *is published weekly
(50 issues), by EIR News Service, Inc.,
P.O. Box 17390, Washington, D.C. 20041-0390.
(703) 297-8434*

European Headquarters: E.I.R. GmbH, Postfach
Bahnstrasse 9a, D-65205, Wiesbaden, Germany
Tel: 49-611-73650
Homepage: http://www.eir.de
e-mail: info@eir.de
Director: Georg Neudecker

Montreal, Canada: 514-461-1557
eir@eircanada.ca

Denmark: EIR - Danmark, Sankt Knuds Vej 11,
basement left, DK-1903 Frederiksberg, Denmark.
Tel.: +45 35 43 60 40, Fax: +45 35 43 87 57. e-mail:
eirdk@hotmail.com.

Mexico City: EIR, Sor Juana Inés de la Cruz 242-2
Col. Agricultura C.P. 11360
Delegación M. Hidalgo, México D.F.
Tel. (5525) 5318-2301
eirmexico@gmail.com

Copyright: ©2017 EIR News Service. All rights
reserved. Reproduction in whole or in part without
permission strictly prohibited.

Canada Post Publication Sales Agreement
#40683579

Postmaster: Send all address changes to *EIR*, P.O.
Box 17390, Washington, D.C. 20041-0390.

Signed articles in *EIR* represent the views of the authors,
and not necessarily those of the Editorial Board.

Lock Up Bob Mueller

Helga Zepp-LaRouche to *Junge Welt:* 'The New Silk Road Was One of Our Ideas'

Sept. 13—*Junge Welt* (Young World), a German daily, published a brief interview with Helga Zepp-LaRouche, chairwoman of the German political party, Civil Rights Movement Solidarity (BüSo) on Sept. 13, under the provocative title, 'The New Silk Road Was One of Our Ideas'—provocative in the current debate over China's New Silk Road in the German Federal election campaign, in which Mrs. Zepp-LaRouche is leading a national slate of candidates. *Junge Welt*, published in Berlin, is a Marxist daily with a readership of 50,000. Without explanation, the interview was taken down from its website the next day.

In the interview, when asked what the BüSo stands for, Zepp-LaRouche replied, "We want a new paradigm in politics—a shift away from geopolitics, to the common aims of mankind. We believe that a continuation of geopolitics holds the danger of confrontation with Russia and China. That is one of the reasons we support the initiative of Xi Jinping to create a New Silk Road on the basis of win-win cooperation among all the nations of the world."

But the New Silk Road is more than a Eurasian concept, she said: "This new

Mittwoch, 13. September 2017, Nr. 213

»Neue Seidenstraße war eine unserer Ideen«

Die »Bürgerrechtsbewegung Solidarität« definiert ihre Rolle anders als andere Kleinparteien. **Gespräch mit Helga Zepp-LaRouche**

BüSo ist für eine Kleinpartei vergleichsweise alt. Die Plakate waren gefühlt immer da. Wofür steht die »Bürgerrechtsbewegung Solidarität«?

Wir wollen ein neues Paradigma in der Politik – weg von der Geopolitik hin zu den gemeinsamen Zielen der Menschheit. Wir sind der Meinung, dass eine Fortsetzung der Geopolitik die Gefahr der Konfrontation mit Russland und China beinhaltet. Das ist einer der Gründe, warum wir die Initiative von Xi Jinping unterstützen, eine neue Seidenstraße zu schaffen auf der Basis einer Win-Win-Kooperation zwischen allen Nationen dieser Welt.

Jetzt würden Transatlantiker einwenden, dass dies nach einer Eurasischen Union klingt. Was halten Sie dem entgegen, oder stimmt das vielleicht sogar?

Das geht weit darüber hinaus. Dieses neue Modell der wirtschaftlichen Ko-

Helga Zepp-LaRouche ist Parteivorsitzende der »Bürgerrechtsbewegung Solidarität«

re Steuergesetzgebung sinnvoll wäre. Was aber drängend ist, ist die Schaffung neuer produktiver Arbeitsplätze, dem könnten wir uns mit dem Projekt der neuen Seidenstraße nähern. Wir müssen zum Beispiel mehr Energie in die Grundlagenforschung stecken, mehr auf die Ausbildung von Avantgardetechnologien setzen. Im Grunde würden wir die Produktivität der gesamten arbeitenden Bevölkerung erhöhen durch diese Art der zukunftsorientierten Kooperation. Wir müssten machen, was China heute tut. Das Land legt großen Wert auf Exzellenz in der Ausbildung, besonders in den Natur- und Ingenieurwissenschaften. Das ist exakt das, was Deutschland zur Zeit des hiesigen Wirtschaftswunders gemacht hat, während wir uns nun leider dem Diktat der Banken unterworfen haben, weshalb diese ganzen Missstände existieren.

model of economic cooperation has found widespread support in Latin America and above all in Africa. That rather obviously goes beyond the scope of a Eurasian Union. The development of Africa, as we see it, is the unique opportunity to solve the refugee crisis on a human basis, by combatting at long last the consequences of colonialism and of the subsequent IMF credit conditionalities. Only the development of infrastructure creates the preconditions for a real development of the entire continent."

China's Economic Miracle

Junge Welt asked about meeting the needs of working people.

Zepp-LaRouche: "In Europe generally, we have the problem of youth unemployment, that has immense consequences even now in southern Europe. When a third of young people are neither working nor studying, it means that they have no future. In Germany too, we have a gigantic problem of poverty, which the government had to admit in its *Report on Poverty*. In the prevailing circumstances, those who have the misfortune to be born into poor families have little opportunity to escape it."

The interviewer aked what kind of redistribution she would like to see.

Zepp-LaRouche: "It is not so much a matter of redistribution, although naturally a different tax law would make sense. But what is urgent is the creation of new, productive jobs, which cooperation with the New Silk Road would help to accomplish. For example, we must invest more energy in fundamental research, and in developing cutting-edge technologies. We would raise the productivity of the entire working population through this kind of future-oriented cooperation. We should do what China is doing now. China gives great importance to excellence in education, especially in the natural sciences and engineering. That is exactly what Germany did to create its Economic Miracle, whereas today, the banks are dictating policy, which is the reason all of these abuses exist."

Junge Welt asked if Zepp-LaRouche thought it was realistic to expect that her ideas would be adopted.

Zepp-LaRouche: "The vision of the New Silk Road was one of our ideas for creating a peaceful world order for the 21st Century. We have worked on for it for 26 years, and the Chinese government fully recognizes our part in this perspective. We are portrayed much more fairly in the press there than in the mainstream press here. Thus we are a party that operates on an entirely different plane than other so-called 'small parties.' And I would hope this will be converted into votes as well."

In concluding, the interviewer asked whether Zepp-LaRouche had been educated as a socialist.

Zepp-LaRouche: "I was educated as a humanist, as a world citizen."

EIR Contents

www.larouchepub.com Volume 44, Number 38, September 22, 2017

White House Photo/Pete Souza

Cover This Week

I. Smash the 'Russiagate' Hoax

Britain Is the Enemy Behind 'Russiagate'

The following is an edited version of remarks delivered by William F. Wertz, Jr. in New York City on September 9, 2017. Wertz' presentation was given in the context of a day-long conference, "The 'Russian Hack' Inside Job: Who's Trying To Destroy The Presidency and Start a World War with Russia?" sponsored by Executive Intelligence Review. *That conference also included presentations given by Ray McGovern and William Binney, both leaders of the Veteran Intelligence Professionals for Sanity (VIPS). See* EIR, Sept. 15, 2017.

Will Wertz: I'd like to start by wishing Lyndon LaRouche a Happy Birthday, which was actually yesterday. It was his 95th birthday. I also want to express my gratitude, the gratitude of the LaRouche movement, for the courageous efforts undertaken by Ray McGovern, and Bill Binney, and the VIPS in the fight for truth. The German poet Friedrich Schiller, in his writing on universal history, said "What greater gift than truth has any man to give to man?" What they have developed in terms of the forensics analysis, which they will present later, is extraordinarily important, because it undermines the entire lie which has been used to mobilize against Russia, against the Presidency of the United States, and against the possibility of a new paradigm for humanity as a whole.

Now, many years ago, actually about 2,500 years ago, Plato wrote two dialogues among others—the *Timaeus* and the *Critias*. What he discusses, in both of those, is a flood which wiped out an entire civilization. In the *Timaeus*, Plato reports that an Egyptian priest said to Solon, "You Hellenes are never anything but children. There is not an old man among you. ... There have

been and will be again, many destructions of mankind arising out of many causes. The greatest have been brought about by the agencies of fire and water." He points out that the reason these civilizations were unable to deal with such natural disasters is that "The gods' part in them began to wax faint ... and they began to behave themselves unseemly. They were taking the infection of wicked coveting and the pride of power." Now fortunately we have in the United States, some old men—particularly Lyndon LaRouche—who, in fact, is younger than most people in terms of his mind.

LaRouche's Fight

What I want to do is to lay out exactly what LaRouche has fought for, in a thumbnail sketch, because I don't have enough time to do this in depth. But Lyndon LaRouche has fought against the British Empire, stemming back at least to his time in World War II on the Indian subcontinent and in Burma, which were part of the British Empire at that time.

He saw first-hand the genocidal policy of the British against the Indian population. At that point, he developed a lifelong commitment to defeating the British

President Franklin Roosevelt (left) making a point to U.K. Prime Minister Winston Churchill at the Yalta conference, Feb. 4, 1945.

Empire, and to doing what Franklin Roosevelt told Winston Churchill during the war that he was committed to doing. Roosevelt said: We are not fighting World War II to preserve the British Empire; after World War II, we are going to use American System methods of economic development to develop the rest of the world.

Unfortunately that mission of Roosevelt was sabotaged after his death by Winston Churchill and by Harry S Truman, a very small-minded man. Instead, the first mobilization against Russia took place, and specifically against the alliance which Roosevelt had been committed to—which was an alliance between the United States, Russia, China, and other nations to develop the planet using American System methods.

Looking at Lyndon LaRouche's fight over a number of decades, I would just point out a few things. First of all, Lyndon LaRouche is an original thinker in the tradition of Nicholas of Cusa, and of Gottfried Leibniz. He's an economist who has correctly forecast economic developments over any number of decades.

• He was alone in forecasting the 1971 end of the Bretton Woods system, a forecast for which he was ridiculed by establishment economists—until it happened. He also foresaw the disastrous results of Nixon's Aug. 15, 1971 action. He has put forward solutions over decades which, if they had been acted upon, would have created a completely different situation on this planet Earth and beyond.

• In 1975, he called for an International Development Bank.

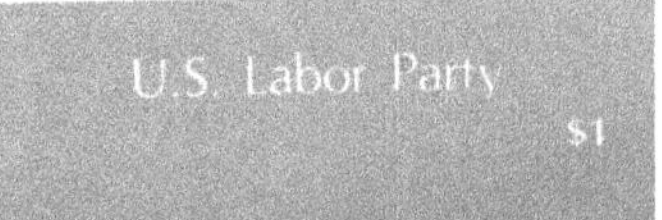

EIRNS/Ruben Cota Meza

Former Mexican President José López Portillo and Helga Zepp-LaRouche, participating in a meeting in Mexico City, Dec. 1, 1998.

• In 1977, he called for a Third National Bank of the United States.

• In the late 1970s, and then into the beginning of the Reagan Administration, he worked for what Reagan later announced in March 1983 as the Strategic Defense Initiative (SDI), as a means of eliminating the danger of thermonuclear war between the United States and Russia.

• In 1982, he called for Operation Juarez, which was to be a model for North-South relations between the United States and Mexico, whereby technology would be transferred to Mexico in exchange for oil, to develop the economy of Mexico. All of the problems that we've had since then, surrounding NAFTA and related issues, are a result of the failure to economically develop Mexico and also Central America.

• In 1983, he put forward a program for the long-term economic development of the Pacific and Indian Ocean Basins.

• In 1990, he and his wife Helga Zepp-LaRouche put forward the idea of the Productive Triangle, which was a concept of economic development corridors between Paris, Berlin, and Vienna. That was later extended, after the fall of the Soviet Union, to a call for a Eurasian Land-Bridge.

• In 1990, he put forward a program called the Oasis Plan, for economic development in the Middle East, which would have been the basis for solving the Israeli-Palestinian crisis.

• In 1997, he called for a New Bretton Woods conference to create a "new financial architecture," as Bill Clinton later called it before

Clinton came under attack. This would have been the basis for economic development throughout the world.

• In 1997, the *EIR* published a special report titled *The Eurasian Land-Bridge: the 'New Silk Road'*. That's 20 years before the development of the One Belt, One Road—the Silk Road policy which is now becoming hegemonic throughout the rest of the world.

The British Hand

I want to focus on the reason there is this present attack on Russia, and why there is an attack on President Trump. I would maintain that the main reason is the anti-Trump role of the British empire, an empire which emphatically does exist; it may exist in a different form than it existed prior to World War II, but it does exist, and it exerts influence throughout the world, and specifically also in the United States.

Dale Creek Bridge during the construction of the Union Pacific Railroad, 1864-1869.

The British have been involved in the attack on Russia and President Trump from the very beginning. It's been documented in the press; there's a *Guardian* article that stated that the Government Communications Headquarters of Britain [GCHQ]—which is their equivalent of the NSA—began to surveil Trump as far back as 2015, just after Trump announced for President. That's back in 2015.

Then came the case of British MI6 agent Christopher Steele, who developed the so-called dossier which has been the roadmap for various intelligence agents in this country who were associated with the Obama Administration and Hillary Clinton, and who have carried out the continuing campaign against Russia and against President Trump.

The basic motivation is to prevent a situation in which Lyndon LaRouche could actually influence the policies of President Trump, as LaRouche influenced and shaped the policies of Reagan in respect to the SDI, and also had the impact of organizing President Clinton to move toward a new financial architecture before he was subjected to an impeachment operation.

An 'Asiatic Grand Central'

What has President Trump done? During the campaign, he made some of his principles very clear. He wants to work with Russia. It would be a good thing to work with Russia to fight terrorism, in particular. He's opposed to regime change policies which had dominated United States policy from the Bush Administration through Obama, and would have been continued under Hillary Clinton.

Additionally, he sent a delegation to Beijing for the One Belt, One Road conference in May. There is at least the potential for President Trump to move the United States into this new geometry of the One Belt, One Road.

In terms of economic policy—and this has not yet been acted on—he expressed his commitment to the American System of political economy in a way in which no other President of the United States has done since Franklin Roosevelt. On October 26, 2016 in Charlotte, North Carolina, he called for a 21st-century Glass-Steagall.

Then, on March 15, after he had become President, in a speech at Willow Run, Michigan, followed by a speech on March 20 in Louisville, Kentucky, and at a speech at the National Republican Congressional Committee on March 21, he called for the American System of Alexander Hamilton, George Washington, and Abraham Lincoln.

He specifically said in the last speech, "Our first Republican President, Abraham Lincoln, ran his first campaign for public office in 1832 when he was only 23 years old. He began by imagining the benefits a railroad could bring to his part of Illinois, without ever having seen a steam-powered train. He had no idea, and yet he

The Trans-Siberian Railway in the Nineteenth Century.

knew what it could be. Thirty years later as President, Lincoln signed the law that built the first Transcontinental Railroad, uniting our country from ocean to ocean."

The Lincoln Transcontinental Railroad was the inspiration for the Trans-Siberian Railroad in Russia. It was also the inspiration for a much broader grand strategy in the 1890s, which was a precursor to what we're seeing today with the One Belt, One Road policy of the Chinese which has also been advocated by Russia. This goes back to the perspective of Gottfried Leibniz, who wrote: "I consider it a singular plan of the fates that humanity's cultivation and refinement should today be concentrated, as it were, in the two extremes of our continent—in Europe, and in China, which adorns the Orient as Europe does the opposite edge of the Earth. Perhaps supreme providence has ordained such an arrangement, so that as the most cultivated and distant people stretch out their arms to each other, those in between may gradually be brought to a better way of life. I do not think it an accident that the Russians, whose vast realm connects Europe with China and who hold sway over the deep barbarian lands of the north by the shore of the frozen ocean, should be led to the emulation of our ways through the strenuous efforts of their present ruler"—referring to Peter I. This conception of Leibniz in the 1600s, of a bridge for humanity from Europe through Russia to China, is what we're actually seeing as a potential right now. And the British want to stop it.

Our enemy has always been the British Empire. We fought a revolution against the British Empire; they burned down the White House in 1812, and they supported the Confederacy in the Civil War. It was the Russians who effectively supported the American Revolution with the League of Armed Neutrality, and it was the Russians, particularly Czar Alexander II, who intervened in the Civil War against the British by sending his fleet to San Francisco and New York, to prevent any further British support for the Confederacy.

In the 1890s, an alliance based on the American System of political economy was developed. It involved the French, the Germans, and the Russians, in particular. First of all, just let me mention Japan. Henry C. Carey, who was an advisor to Abraham Lincoln, sent one of his colleagues, E. Peshine Smith, to Japan, and introduced American System economic policies, which contributed to the Meiji Restoration. In the 1890s, Gabriel Hanotaux, who was the Foreign Minister of France, put forward a policy he called the "Asiatic Grand Central."

This is his later description of it in retrospect: "Starting from Orenburg on the River Ural, this railroad

Gabriel Hanotaux

would have gone as far as Peshawar on the Indian frontier; joining the Russian system to the Anglo-Indian system of railways across central Asia. It would have been the communication between the Trans-Siberian on the one hand, and the Baghdad Railroad on the other"—which was being built by Germany from Berlin to Baghdad. "The object was to join European railways with the Anglo-Indian railways and beyond, with future Chinese railroads."

At the same time, Count Witte in 1892 became effectively the Transport Minister of Russia, and then later in the year, Finance Minister. He envisioned "A new path and new horizons, not only for Russia but for world trade." This is the Trans-Siberian railroad. "It would rank as one of those world events that usher in new epochs in the history of nations, and not infrequently bring about the radical upheaval of established economic relations between states. And would, particularly in relation to the Asian nations, provide the basis of recognition of tangible, mutual interests in the field of worldwide economic activity of mankind."

This is also the conception of President Xi Jinping of China today: a "win-win" approach, based on mutual interests. It was also the American policy of John Quincy Adams, to create a community of interests among a family of sovereign nation-states.

The British Empire Is the Enemy

At that time the British moved in to kill this whole perspective. And that's precisely what they're attempting to do now.

At that time, specifically, in Germany, Bismarck was forced out in 1890; in 1892, Jules Ferry, who was a mentor of Hanotaux, was assassinated. Sadi Carnot, the

Sergei Witte

President of France, was assassinated June 1894. McKinley was assassinated 1901. And Witte was dismissed in 1903. This is precisely the kind of regime-change policy which the British and their agents in the United States are attempting against the U.S. Presidency today, in order to prevent this kind of—as Hanotaux said at that time—"Asiatic Grand Central." But now we're talking about a World Land-Bridge.

There were additional moves by the British at that point. For instance, on July 16, 1894, the Anglo-Japanese Treaty of Commerce and Navigation was signed, which was to go into force on July 17, 1899—five years later. But within two weeks of the signing of that treaty—on August 1, 1894—the Sino-Japanese War was launched, which was centered on Korea. Many of the problems that we have today in the Korean Peninsula, date back to this whole operation by the British.

In 1895, the Japanese seized Taiwan. Then the Commerce and Navigation Treaty was further developed in 1902, with the Anglo-Japanese alliance that was signed

T. Dart Walker

The assassination of President William McKinley at the Pan-American Exposition reception, Sept. 6, 1901.

Imperial Japanese Navy General Staff

Japanese bombardment of the Russian fleet at Port Arthur the day before the formal declaration of war between Russia and Japan.

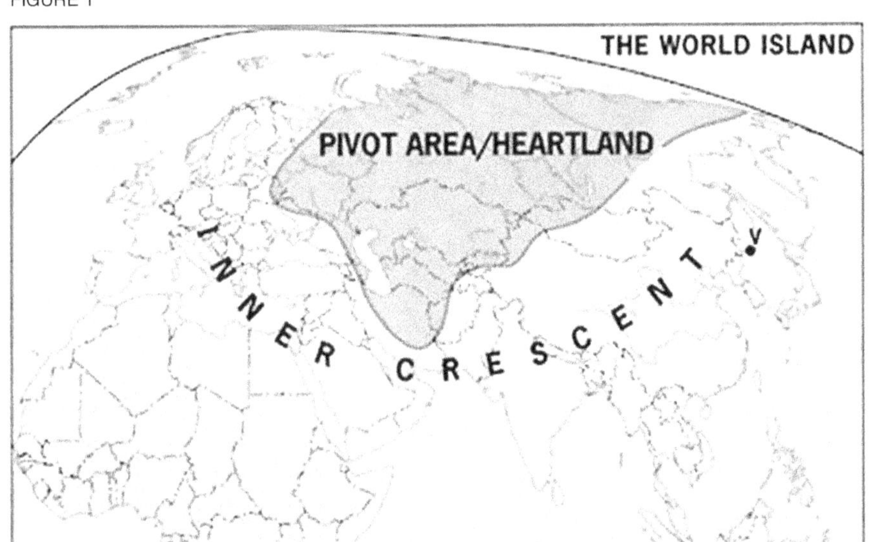

Sir Halford Mackinder's Heartland concept.

on January 30. After Hanotaux had been removed from office, the British also moved forward to create the Entente Cordiale between Britain and France in 1903-04. Then there was the first Russian Revolution in 1905, and then the Triple Entente involving Russia, Britain, and France in 1907.

With the killing of McKinley, Teddy Roosevelt came to office in the United States, and the close relationship between the United States, Germany, and Russia which existed under McKinley was completely reversed. Teddy Roosevelt went in the direction of a special relationship between the United States and Britain, our enemy.

It is probably not insignificant that Teddy Roosevelt's uncle, James Bullock, had been in exile in Britain ever since he was the foreign agent for the Confederacy during the Civil War. This was the source of Teddy Roosevelt's pro-British policy.

So what I'm suggesting here is that we see, at that time, a direct example of how the British Empire operates. That policy was further developed in 1928. This is a geopolitical map [**Figure 1**] that was produced by the British geo-politician Halford Mackinder. The basic idea was to look at Europe, Africa, and Asia, as the world island. The British policy was to surround what they called the pivot area or the heartland, which is Russia, with an inner crescent.

The basic theme of Mackinder was that "Who rules East Europe, commands the heartland. Who rules the heartland, commands the world island. Who rules the world island, commands the world." This was their geopolitical strategy; this is the strategy which was also developed by Haushofer under Hitler, and resulted in the Nazis' project for an attack on Russia, which was supported by the British until Hitler turned west as well.

But if you look at this map, think in terms of the eastward movement of NATO in Europe. Think of the crisis on the Korean Peninsula today. Think of Afghanistan, previously and also today. Think of the Arab Spring and the regime-change policies carried out by Bush and Obama in Iraq, in Libya, the attempt in Syria, and the attempt in Egypt. This is the policy which is still hegemonic even after the fall of the Soviet Union. It is this policy which must be defeated. It is possible that President Trump will move against this, and will actually work with Russia and China for a revival of the Eurasian Land-Bridge conception.

A Grand Strategy for Peace

It's very important that people understand the nature of the grand strategy which Lyndon LaRouche has been committed to, and what his wife Helga Zepp-LaRouche is committed to—a grand strategy for humanity, as against the oligarchical principle of the British empire, where for us, economic development is the basis for peace. It's the basis for cooperation among different nations throughout the world. It's John Quincy Adams' conception of a community of principle among a family of sovereign nation-states, where man can actually then carry out his mission, which is not only to develop the planet for man, but also to explore and colonize space.

Going back to the *Critias* and the *Timaeus,* which I mentioned at the beginning, the point is that man is confronted with floods, he's confronted with fire—and in this case with hurricanes. The basic point is that there are acts of omission and acts of commission which result in a destruction of humanity. The acts of omission include not building the infrastructure that could actually mitigate hurricanes and so forth. There's an act of omission, if you don't work with Russia and China on a joint strategy to prevent asteroids striking the Earth.

Then there are also acts of commission, which include unjust wars—which is fire, thermonuclear fire. There are also acts of commission, including financial policies which are designed from the standpoint of enforcing zero economic growth and population reduction, which have been the policy of the British Empire.

I think, as Lyndon LaRouche has said, victory is within our reach, if we move right now, because we now have a different situation than in the 1890s and the beginning of the 1900s. That situation resulted in over a hundred years of war—two world wars, and then perpetual warfare, with short breaks, after World War II.

Today we have the potential to actually win, and the basic point is we have to break out now and seize the moment to put together an alliance, which LaRouche has called the Four Powers—the United States, Russia, China, India—to defeat the British empire. This would be a liberation of the people of the United Kingdom. It's not aimed at the British people. In the United States, we have to move with what LaRouche has called the Four Laws: This is a policy of Glass-Steagall, national banking, in the sense of Roosevelt's Reconstruction Finance Corporation and Hamilton's National Bank, to issue credit for economic development. We cannot operate from the standpoint of the miserly conception that "we can't spend the money to save people." We've spent trillions to save bankrupt banks! We spend trillions to carry out unjust regime-change wars. What we need to do is to invest in people: Save the people, and cancel the British system.

Discussion: Victory Is Within Reach

Question: As far back as the late 1800s, in China, after China was beaten by Great Britain in the Second Opium War, I think Lincoln sent as his ambassador a man by the name of Burlingame, and then later Wharton Barker, to help with the development of the railway in China. I know that the great Dr. Sun Yat-sen, in 1907, wrote *The International Development of China*, which was the roadmap for developing China's industrial and economic capability. So all the railways, all the waterways, everything that China is now today doing, come from blueprints from Dr. Sun, and essentially—it seems to me—from Lincoln.

Can you comment on the future of potential collaboration between China and the United States, and the collaboration around infrastructure development?

Wertz: What you developed is precisely the case. For instance, the entire plan of Hanotaux and of Witte, was to make sure that the trans-Siberian Railroad actually went through Manchuria. The basic idea was to free China from the British. There were two Opium Wars in the 1800s, prior to this period; there was also a brief war between the French and the Chinese in the Vietnam area. Sun Yat-sen is another reflection of exactly how Lincoln's policy was spread, in terms of the ideas, through Europe, Russia, China, and other locations.

The irony is that China has actually been engaged in precisely what Franklin Roosevelt was committed to: To develop the world through American methods, like the Tennessee Valley Authority, or the Grand Coulee Dam, the locks in the St. Lawrence Seaway, or the Boulder Dam, and the Four Corners policy of Franklin Roosevelt. He wanted to spread this throughout the world. And that was based upon Alexander Hamilton. Graham Lowry's book discusses this: The British did not want the United States to move west, to develop the continent as a whole. And this was the perspective of the Founding Fathers—to move west, and eventually this was consolidated with the Transcontinental Railroad of Lincoln.

The basic point here, as Lyndon LaRouche said the other day, is that victory is within reach. Because we do have some adults who are creative in leadership positions in the world today, which has not always been the case. There was a recent article in the *China Daily*, which featured an interview with Helga Zepp-LaRouche. She reported that she had gone to China back in the 1970s during the Cultural Revolution, and saw the devastation that existed there. And then she returned much later with the perspective of the Silk Road. And there's an appreciation in China of the role that the LaRouches, and particularly Helga in terms of China, have played.

You see what Lyndon LaRouche has done, really from the 1970s. He wasn't just concerned about the United States. He functioned, as Schiller said, "as a patriot of his own country, but also as a citizen of the world." He was elaborating programs for development for the entire world, in the spirit of what Franklin Roosevelt told Winston Churchill that America was going to do, as opposed to what the British Empire wanted to do.

That is where we are today, and I would just say, as I stressed, this is what's at stake right now. It's really up to, in this country, the American people—but obviously throughout the world, for people to really understand this: that you've got rise to the level of grand strategy, of a grand design for the world, for humanity as a whole.

The World Land-Bridge Network—Key Links and Corridors

*Committed, underway or completed

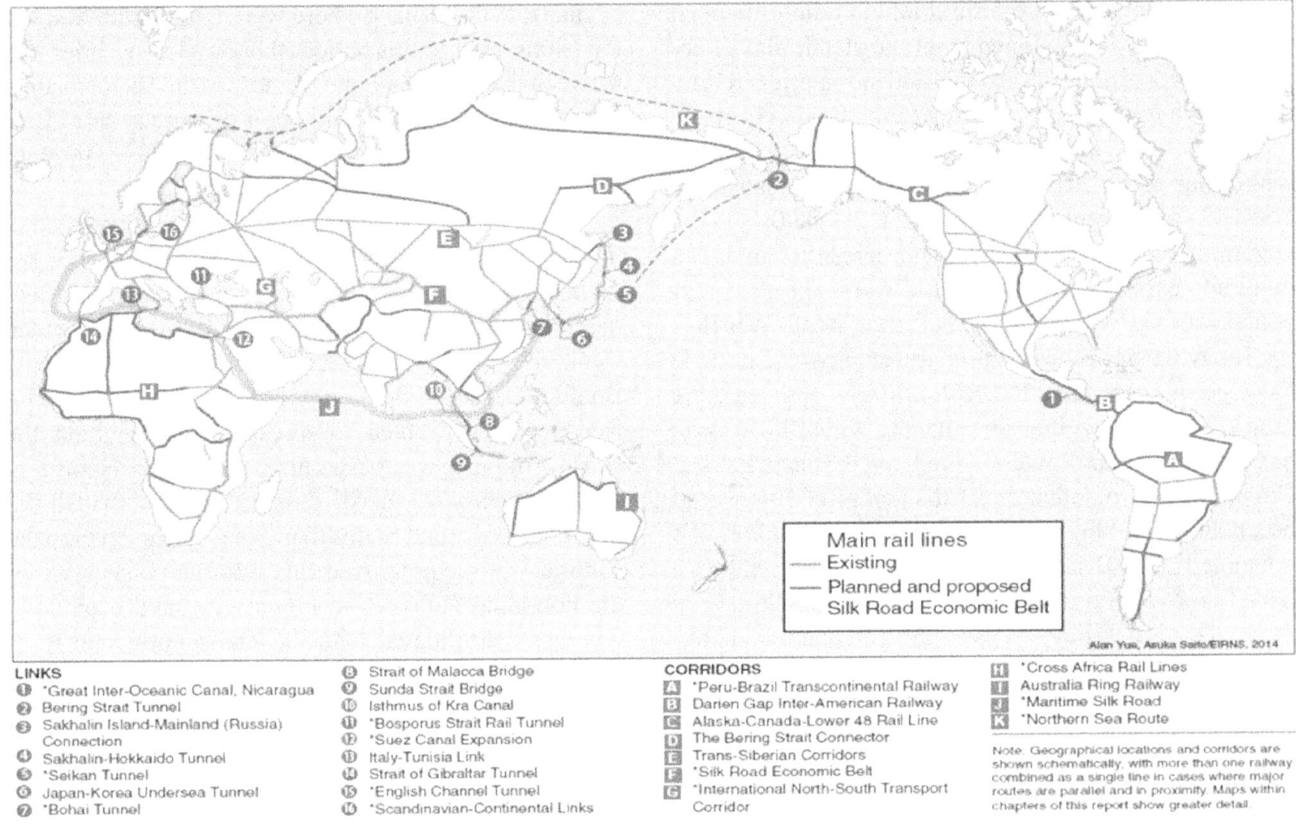

LINKS

1. *Great Inter-Oceanic Canal, Nicaragua
2. Bering Strait Tunnel
3. Sakhalin Island-Mainland (Russia) Connection
4. Sakhalin-Hokkaido Tunnel
5. *Seikan Tunnel
6. Japan-Korea Undersea Tunnel
7. *Bohai Tunnel
8. Strait of Malacca Bridge
9. Sunda Strait Bridge
10. Isthmus of Kra Canal
11. *Bosporus Strait Rail Tunnel
12. *Suez Canal Expansion
13. Italy-Tunisia Link
14. Strait of Gibraltar Tunnel
15. *English Channel Tunnel
16. *Scandinavian-Continental Links

CORRIDORS

A. *Peru-Brazil Transcontinental Railway
B. Darien Gap Inter-American Railway
C. Alaska-Canada-Lower 48 Rail Line
D. The Bering Strait Connector
E. Trans-Siberian Corridors
F. *Silk Road Economic Belt
G. *International North-South Transport Corridor
H. *Cross Africa Rail Lines
I. Australia Ring Railway
J. *Maritime Silk Road
K. *Northern Sea Route

Note: Geographical locations and corridors are shown schematically, with more than one railway combined as a single line in cases where major routes are parallel and in proximity. Maps within chapters of this report show greater detail.

You've got to approach it from that standpoint. Yes, fight for your own people, but you also have to fight for humanity as a whole—and it has to be based on truth and the question of justice.

And I think that's really the issue, and we've got to mobilize to make sure that this succeeds at this moment.

Question: I'm from New York. One of my many interests in this world is to remind people that they can think for themselves. They don't need a media outlet to tell them what to think. I'm in the business of teaching people how to think. So, it pains me, not as just an educator but as a human being, when I see other Americans hoodwinked by things like Russia-gate. When you look at just New York City alone, we have a failing infrastructure, with a subway system that is overcrowded and over-packed. We have roads that people can't even drive on any longer—and yet people care about how many scoops of ice cream Trump gets every day. So, the essential question here is, how do we make sure that this is the last time a Russia-gate happens, so that people can now, instead of talking about themselves, or worry-ing about what their President eats—they can worry about fixing their own country, fixing their own state, ensuring that people can be educated—the real issues?

Wertz: I think the American poet Edgar Allan Poe addressed the issue most directly in a short story called "Mellonta Tauta," because what he said there is that the oligarchy is able to control a population to the extent to which it is convinced that there are only two pathways to truth—empiricism and logical deduction. If you look at all of the things that we've been confronted with over the recent period, that's precisely the way in which people have been brainwashed. They look at the empirical evidence which they've been fed by the media, by so-called authorities, and they operate from the standpoint of certain logical deductive axioms. And they're trapped in this situation.

But Poe basically said that the empiricist's method is the Baconian method. He was referring to Francis Bacon, and the logical deductive method is that of Aristotle, to whom he referred. To be human, he said, is not to creep or crawl, as you would from the standpoint of empiricism or logical deduction; but rather to soar and to use the method of hypothesis, which is the method of Plato, of creative thinking. He said this method is the method of Kepler, and that is the real critical issue. *People have to understand how to think.* If you think that the only way that you come to knowledge is through empiricism or logical deduction, then you're controlled by the oligarchy. This is a fundamental principle that people have to actually understand.

We have reason to be optimistic, because the world has a very clear alternative, represented by a New Paradigm. To the extent to which you see people responding, for instance in the face of these hurricanes, in a manner which is similar to that of the Good Samaritan—that is what makes us human. Just to reflect on what you were saying—it is a passion for the truth, a commitment to humanity. It's what the Greeks called agapē, or love. It's that quality that is evident in the situation in many sections of the world today.

Look at the win-win strategy that was put forward by the Chinese—this is the strategy that ended the Thirty Years War in Europe in the 1600s. It was the concept of the Treaty of Westphalia, to act on the basis of the benefit of the other, as opposed to egoism. I think this is also what the poet Percy Bysshe Shelley referred to in his *A Defence of Poetry*; it's a kind of mass-strike phenomenon, which is not an economic strike or a general strike. It's a mental process in which people rise above their parochial interests and think about humanity as a whole. What we require right now is to really elevate the kind of good works that you see—such as in people risking their lives to save other people in the case of Texas; or what we saw with the first responders on 9/11. We have to actually rise to the level of "what do we need to do for humanity right now?" Think in those terms, which is to think big, in terms of what the mission of man is. And I think if we do that, then we have the potential for bringing about a very fundamental change right now.

President Trump could take certain actions right now. The "Russia-gate" is blown out of the water by the evidence that has been presented here today. He should seize the moment, not just to raise the debt ceiling, but rather to move with his promises during and after the election, and to work with China and Russia to eliminate the danger of thermonuclear war, and to join in the fight against terrorism, which the Russians have advocated repeatedly. That's the direction in which we have to go. That will bring about a complete shift in the world as we know it.

The Fraud of the Russian Hack, and How 9/11 Could Have Been Prevented

by Dennis Speed

Sept. 18—William Binney's presentation to the 140 persons attending the September 9 Manhattan *EIR* conference, "The 'Russian Hack' Inside Job: Who's Trying To Destroy the Presidency and Start a World War with Russia?" contained not one, but two explosive revelations regarding the practice of disinformation and obfuscation carried out by various "national security" agencies against the American people over the past twenty years. While the forum was devoted to disproving the now thoroughly discredited "Russian hack" story, Binney, a thirty-plus year veteran of the National Security Agency (NSA)

William Binney (left) and Ray McGovern, both of the Veteran Intelligence Professionals for Sanity, addressed the Sept. 9 EIR conference in New York.

who resigned in disgust in October 2001, besides demolishing the "Russiagate" hoax, revealed to the astonished audience that security systems he had designed prior to 9/11 would have prevented that attack from occurring, had he and his associates not been deliberately prevented from deploying them by others at the NSA.

Instead, Binney asserted, universal surveillance capabilities that he personally designed to protect Americans from terrorist attack, were deployed after 9/11 to monitor virtually every citizen of the United States who has an electronic device.

Ray McGovern, Binney's colleague in the Veteran Intelligence Professionals for Sanity (VIPS), also addressed the conference.

Binney's revelation was not beside the point, especially when presented to New Yorkers on the weekend of the 16th anniversary of 9/11, the September 11, 2001 killing of 3,000 persons at the World Trade Center's

North and South towers, which, together with World Trade Center Building 7, disintegrated that day. It was not beside the point, given that, were the contention proven true—as it indeed was again, in the course of Binney's presentation—that the so-called "Russian hack of the DNC" was in fact an inside job, it would be not only reasonable but necessary to conclude that the continuing irresponsible scapegoating of Russia, for whatever reason, by media, the legal system, and political figures is in fact intended to provoke war, including possible thermonuclear war, perhaps with Russia, perhaps with China, just as the 9/11 attacks had ensured war in their immediate aftermath.

There is a precedent in recent American history for the use of multiply connected agencies, private and governmental, to carry out such illegal operations. In his introduction of the panel that day, moderator Dennis Speed pointed out that the same criminal elements involved in the attempt to overthrow the Presidency of the United States today—including former FBI Director Robert Mueller, for example—were also involved in the 1987 prosecution of Lyndon LaRouche. That prosecution was characterized in September 1994 by former Attorney General Ramsey Clark as representing "a broader range of deliberate cunning and systematic misconduct over a longer period of time utilizing the power of the federal government, than any other prosecution by the U.S. Government in my time or to my knowledge."

LaRouche, who had acted as a back channel negotiator with the then Soviet Union on behalf of the policy that became known in 1983 as the Strategic Defense Initiative, was at that time feared by his policy enemies, according to a former Reagan Administration staffer participating in the September 9 meeting as "the most dangerous man in the world."

The fact that Robert Mueller, FBI Director on September 11, 2001, has in recent days come under renewed scrutiny in the press for his role in then preventing the follow-up of crucial "9/11" leads (including by the FBI itself), and that Mueller is also now at the center of the "Russia probe of the Trump Administration," is ominously consistent with the crimes that have been committed by a British-manipulated "treason faction" for some time inside the United States. That "Tory faction" has often condemned the United States to self-destructive perpetual war. But the "systemic misconduct" in criminal investigations and prosecutions, perpetrated either to prevent discovery of the authors of a crime, as in 2001, or to perpetrate one, as seen in today's Russia-gate hacking hoax, did not begin with 9/11, but extends back at least to the criminal prosecution of Lyndon LaRouche and his associates from 1984 to 1987 and after.

Referencing LaRouche's celebration of his 95th birthday September 8, Speed said at the outset that *Executive Intelligence Review* was "founded in 1974 by Lyndon LaRouche, an economist, statesman and philosopher, as well as lifelong political opponent of the British Financial Intelligence Establishment. Yesterday, despite his lifelong enemies, Mr. LaRouche celebrated his 95th birthday. The *EIR* has distinguished itself by employing a unique investigative method that

Firefighters and urban search and rescue teams work amidst the rubble of the collapsed World Trade Center in Manhattan, Sept. 16, 2001.

… has been brought by LaRouche to an extraordinarily high level of refinement as a scientific tool. As a friend of mine (the late biographer, Russian expert, and acquaintance of Albert Einstein), Paul Robeson, Jr., said to me after meeting Mr. LaRouche in 2008, 'Lyndon LaRouche is to economic analysis what Einstein is to physics.' "

Intelligence Is Determined by Method

The underlying topic, the "substrate" of the day's symposium was, in fact, a dialogue on scientific method and its application to crime solving. Schiller translator and LaRouche associate William Wertz's presentation (in the preceding article in this issue) had used Schiller's method of universal history to establish British authorship of the recent Russia hoax. He situated today's events in the centuries-old British hostility to the development of Gottfried Leibniz's proposal for East-West win-win cooperation, and the round of assassinations and "regime changes" carried out by London's Prince Albert (later Edward VII) in Germany, France, Russia, and the United States, to prevent what has now once again emerged through the efforts of China, Russia, and Lyndon and Helga Zepp-LaRouche.

In his introduction to Binney, who spoke next, Speed pointed to Binney's thought process, rather than the mere "agency" collection of information, to distinguish between what is properly called intelligence, and what is mere "trash collection." One of the things that distinguishes him is that, in his design of the particular system called ThinThread, when he was confronted by the concept which seemed by many to be very daunting, of "how do you monitor two and a half billion electronic units globally in real time," he said, "Well, you think about it as being instantaneous—there's only a certain finite number of atoms in the universe at any instantaneous moment."

Speed referred to Binney's own statement, taken from a recent documentary. "My philosophy was very simple. If somebody said that something was impossible, that's something you have to do. It's like open-ended thinking. You don't bound your thinking. You let it float anywhere it wants to go. So that gives you the idea how you can be creative in any environment. And so I—that's what I was after: being creative anywhere I went. And that's what the SARC—the Sigint [Signals Intelligence] Automation Research Center—was all about."

Such insight allowed Binney to think in ways unavailable to others, and therefore to solve problems they could not see, much less solve. William Binney and his SARC were able to design ThinThread to meet that impossible requirement. This meant, as he recounted in the film *A Good American*, "building relationships among billions of people. I mean, we were talking trillions of transactions. It was pretty clear that we were building the most powerful analysis tool that had been developed in history, to monitor, basically, the entire world, in near-real time. This is monitoring every member of the population automatically...."

Binney described his failed attempt to deploy his system on behalf of NSA's sworn mission to protect the American people in these words, featured in the just-mentioned 2015 documentary directed by Friedrich Moser, *A Good American*, only released recently in the United States:

"We decided to continue developing ThinThread to try to ensure that we had something that would functionally work by the end of 2000 so that we could address the terrorism problem in the real world—not in the wish world of [the inferior system] Trailblazer, for example. That's when I went to our Terrorism Analysis Center and said, okay, what sites do you have that produce any meaningful information for you to analyze the terrorism targets around the world? So they gave me a list of eighteen sites. So I took that as a target set to go against terrorism. And then I came in November of 2000, and made a proposal that we do a deployment of ThinThread to those 18 sites, starting in January of 2001. But it came back rejected. So I don't know exactly who rejected it. I assume it was the chief of

Greeting from Virginia State Senator Richard Black

Virginia State Senator Richard Black sent the following greeting to William Binney, Ray McGovern, and other conference participants at the EIR Sept. 9 conference in New York City.

Sept. 7, 2017

The Veteran Intelligence Professionals for Sanity (VIPS) has presented evidence to President Trump that Russia never hacked the Democratic National Committee. The VIPS's review of the matter strongly raises the likelihood that the emails in question were leaked by an insider, not hacked, and were subsequently altered to attribute responsibility to Russia. I am in agreement that a new special prosecutor should be appointed to investigate those responsible for perpetrating the possible hoax which has so damaged and divided our entire nation. I urge President Trump to act on your suggestion, and I support your steadfast efforts to bring the truth to light.

Richard H. Black
Senator of Virginia
13th District

CID—Maureen Baginski. She was the third person in rank in the Agency. There was the Director, then the Deputy Director, then her ...

"On 9/11, I had taken my father-in-law to the eye doctor for an examination; so I was sitting in the waiting room, watching television while he was getting examined. And that's when I saw the first plane hit the tower in New York. And immediately that said to me that we as an agency had failed to give warning of this terrorist attack...."

Thomas Drake, who took over the running of Thin-Thread after Binney's departure, decided to run the Thinthread program after the fact, to determine whether there was valuable intelligence already in the NSA database that ThinThread could identify. He stated in the *Good American* film that "we let ThinThread run—it was somewhere around 24 and 36 hours. I remember our program manager coming back with the initial results. And they were just devastating.

"We discovered critical intelligence—Al-Qaeda and associated movement and intelligence that had never been discovered by NSA. They didn't even know they had it in their databases. But also the specific details of numbers and movement and times and locations, travel—and you're seeing the dispersal patterns that occurred after it happened. You're also seeing that there were parts of the plot in which they weren't successful. There were multiple planes that had been targeted ... And for a number of reasons, those particular planes were not actually hijacked. You can imagine the horror of realizing what had not been discovered, and the confirmation of what was known, sitting in these databases. What if this was discovered prior to 9/11? We had the information in the databases. NSA'S response? Completely shut the program down."

The program as designed was shut down. Then the very same program that Binney and his SIGINT team had refined and perfected, was instead used to monitor everyone in the United States. It was when he discovered that his system was being used for this purpose, without him, his team, and against his will, that William Binney decided he had no recourse except to leave the NSA and begin the process in which he is now engaged—exposing the actions of fraud, including the recent Russia-gate deployed against the President of the United States, as the only honorable means available to him to carry out his oath to protect the citizens of the United States from enemies foreign and domestic.

His and Ray McGovern's VIPS had attempted to warn about the "weapons of mass destruction" hoax (itself inspired by the British Downing Street Memo and the "Niger yellowcake" hoax), prior to the 2003 Iraq War. They and others failed at that time. Now, with the danger of thermonuclear conflict looming, failure is truly not an option.

What follows is an extended excerpt from Binney's remarks. The entire speech can be seen here.

William Binney: "Thank you. Thank you. And thanks for inviting me here. It's a pleasure to be here. I should tell you a little about my background, so you can understand where I'm coming from. I basically was one of the main people, or one of several main people at NSA, and in the intelligence community doing warnings against the Soviet Union. And so, I learned very clearly that whatever you did or said in relation to warning, had to be *right*. You could not be wrong, because this was really a serious issue. People could be vaporized as a result. So you had to know and be sure of what you were doing."

Binney created an independent working concept of how to assess real national threat conditions by developing a system of indicators that contrasted multiple intelligence evaluations and their collection methods, as well as their change over time:

"As part of that process, I built up a way of just thinking about how to verify and validate things, from multiple sources, or from over time, and based on my knowledge of how [intelligence sources] operate, and the existence of my better understanding of what really meant warning, which the entire intelligence community didn't have. I had five warning indicators, which I discussed a little bit in the movie, but I didn't say what they were—because I can't. But the point was, they were the only five meaningful warning indicators, and there are over a hundred-some on the warning list in the Pentagon. None of the five were there. So, it basically said, people didn't really understand what they were doing. It was a matter of trying to figure out how can I verify this entire process and be right in what I said to people, with back-up of basic facts that would indicate these are the things they are doing or are intending to do."

Believing Is Not Necessarily Knowing

"So I was always a factually-based person. So, in other words, I had to have something to factually ground what I was saying; otherwise, I didn't say it, because it was pure speculation at that point. And anybody's speculation is as good as anybody else's. Emotions can come in, and emotions can change expectations and beliefs and so on. And so you could speculate any way you wanted at that point; it was meaningless. So, in other words I didn't want to waste my mental energy on meaningless activities. So that was the founding principle that I used to verify and validate what I was doing, all through the years that I was there. And fortunately so, because I wanted to make sure that the government of the United States didn't have a false statement or false grounding to make a bad decision, because it could be very serious and bad for the country and bad for the people of the world.

"So, that was my founding, and when I first heard about this Russia-gate and Russia was doing this, I was listening to the news, just like everybody else. And the way they came across, saying, 'we have high confidence that this is what they did'—OK: I knew immediately what that meant. That meant they're lying to us. This is called a 'wild-ass guess.' Because they fundamentally didn't know. Of course, you see, I designed a lot of programs they currently are using to spy on everybody—not intentionally, but they subverted it to do that."

Don't Bury Intelligence in Data

Binney recognized that intelligence and "information"—data—are two completely different things, which can even be opposites.

"And that's fundamentally what the movie [*A Good American*] is about. It's about how to design a system to monitor the entire world and pick out—the whole idea, back then, we were facing terrorism, all kinds of criminal activity in the world, and the explosion of the digital communications, in terms of phones, and email, and so on. So the question was, how could you design a system to figure out what's going on in the world and only pull out the data that's relevant to target what you want to analyze; and not take in the entire data of the world, because at that point you're buried. And that's fundamentally what they did, so that's why they can't figure out anything now—they're buried!

"And people like Clapper and others come out—and I know them personally, by the way—they come out and say, 'We need to collect more intelligence.' Now, collection is intelligence, in their mind. Well, to me, that's only data, that doesn't mean anything. Only when you understand what you collected can you produce intelligence. It's like, I collect books; I build a library. What's in the library? Do I understand? No! I haven't read all the books.

"That's the stupidity of what's going on here. But it costs a lot of money to do this—a lot of money. They spent almost $1 trillion on intelligence, just intelligence, since 9/11. That's $1 trillion of the $20 trillion that we have now in our debt. So, when they said that, I knew immediately this was false. You know, the Russians,— Obviously, they have no idea who did it, but they wanted to create an agenda. And they had an agenda driving them and they wanted to create a narrative and manipulate people, and give disinformation. And the Russians did the same thing; every country in the world does the same thing—they call it *desinformatsia*, *manipulatsia*, things like that. Every country does it.

"But coming in and hacking into the DNC, I knew they had no evidence whatsoever, and the question was, can we on the outside, without having access to the collection data, can we figure it out? Well, I went on television at the time, in August of last year, saying that this was false, because if it was true, NSA would have it and they would know exactly who did it. And the reason I know that NSA would have it, is because of these programs."

We, Not Terrorists, Are the Target

When Binney provided the *New York Times* with hard evidence that the United States intelligence agencies were engaged in universal, unconstitutional surveillance against the entire American population, "the Gray Lady," the "national newspaper of record" turned yellow, and refused to record the facts.

"These are the tapping points inside the U.S. as of 2004. [**Fig. 1**] Thirteen years ago, these were the tap points. Now I know exactly where every tap point is, down to the building. I don't know what floor in the building, but I know it's this building. I gave these to Laura Poitras [director of the film, *Citizenfour*], with the hope that they would get published, informing the U.S. public where they were being spied from, and she gave them to the *New York Times*. They would not publish. The reason they didn't publish, is because they said, 'Well, if somebody attacks one of these sites, then we'll be to blame.' So much for informing the U.S. public of what's going on.

"What this really means is [the points are] distrib-

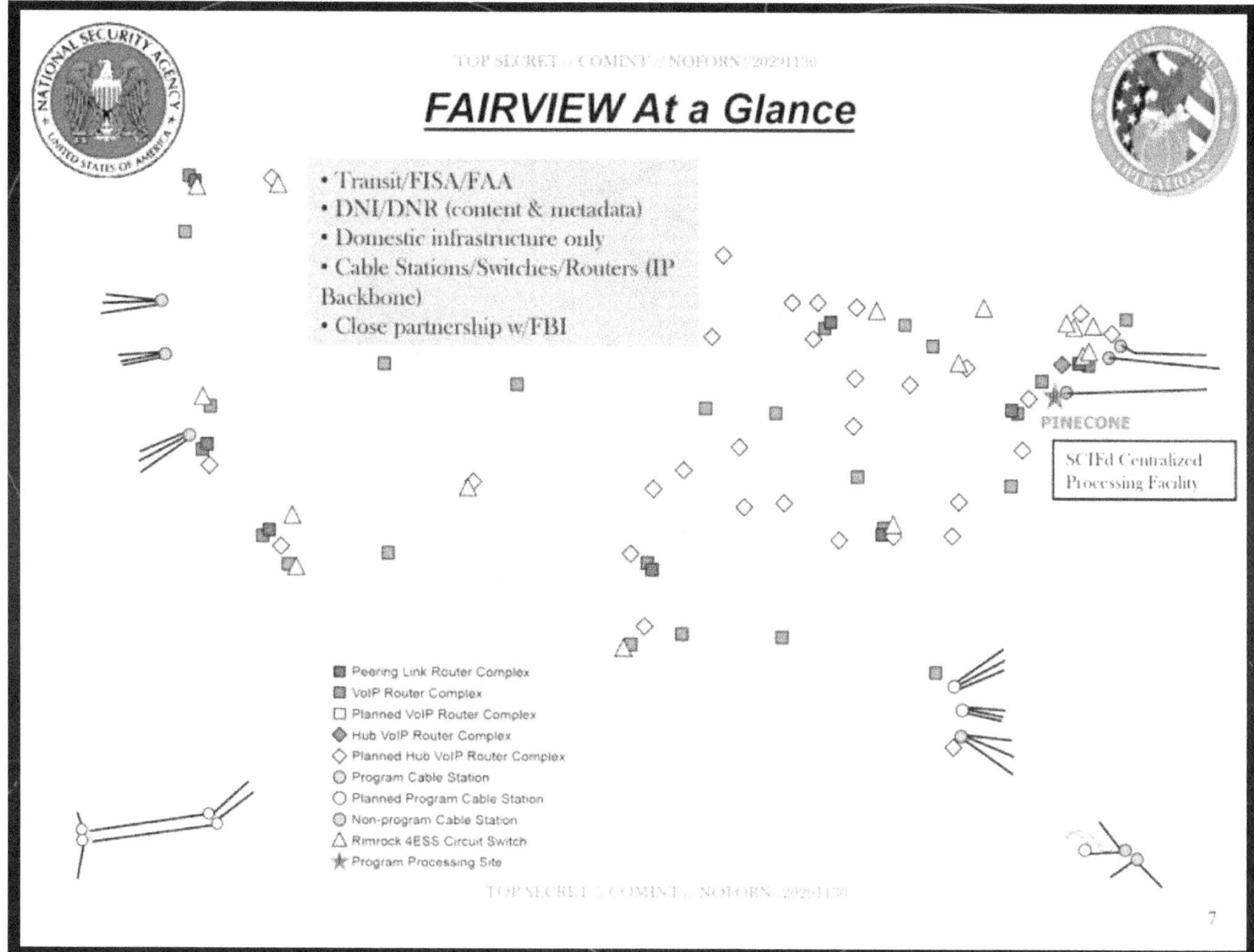

uted with the population of the United States. *We* are the target. If they were after foreigners—you see the little dots on the corner there, the little green ones on the coast? That's where the transoceanic cables come up. And that's where all the foreigners are. So if they were going to collect for foreigners, they'd be at those little green dots, and nowhere else."

Binney demonstrated that between the unacknowledged universal surveillance used domestically against the American people, and the international universal surveillance deployed against everyone else, there was no way for any foreign service, including the Russians, to carry out a "hack" without prior or real-time knowledge of that fact.

"So this is one of the first indications; this is where they get it first. The DNC [hack] would've been picked up by somebody, one of those tapping points. This is, by the way, AT&T. All the buildings are AT&T buildings.

And I did, in mathematical terms—I'm a mathematician, you'll have to excuse me—I had to do a mapping that matched the cluster grouping and cluster mapping of the color code of these tap points with the facilities of AT&T, and *they match perfectly*. So the random probability of that being somebody else other than AT&T is about zero. [laughter] That meant to me, I had it right, it was correct. And plus WikiLeaks said it, too. I wanted to prove it, of course, mathematically. So this is just inside the United States. This is just the first net that's going to catch anything going out of the DNC, or Podesta's server, or anybody's server inside the United States, this is the first set of tapping points where they will pick up all this data....

"At any, rate this is just inside the United States. Around the world it gets even worse [**Fig. 2**]. Because out there, there's no distinction whatsoever; they go through anything unilaterally they want to. If you

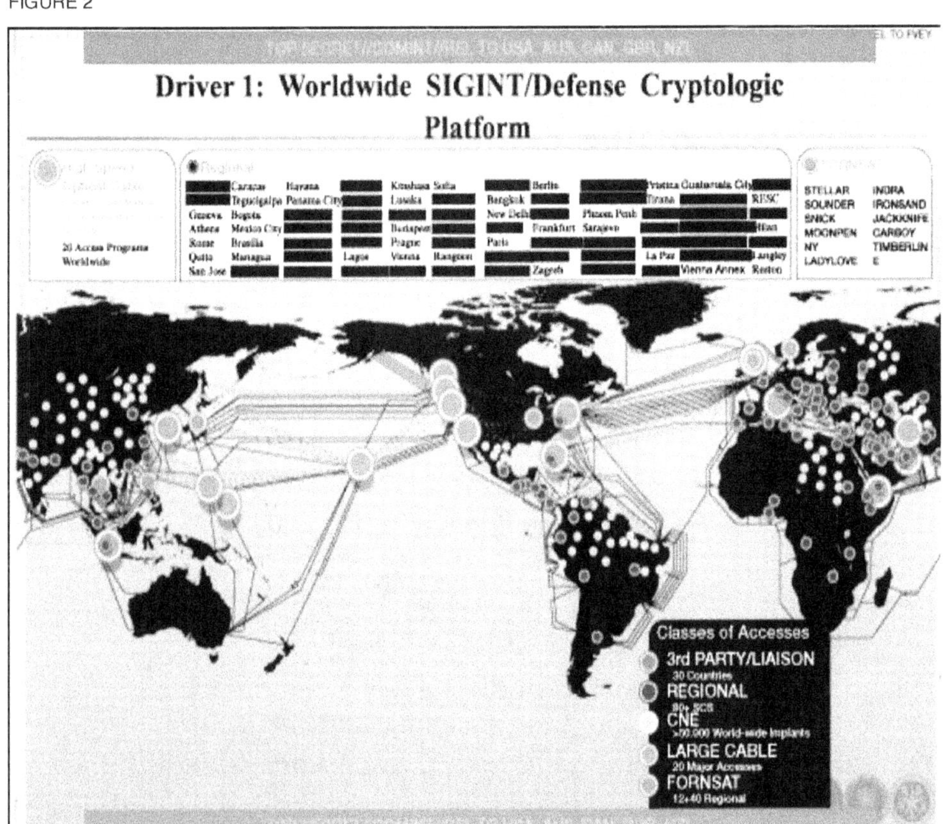

notice, down in the lower right-hand corner, the real important one there is the CNE, greater than 50,000 implants. This is about five or six years ago, at least. CNE is Computer Network Exploitation, and implants, that means software and/or hardware—implants into switches, servers, routers, around the world where they control that router, and they control that server. So that means that anybody sending anything—I mean, Chancellor Merkel didn't have to be in Germany to be collected on her cell phone; she could have been in Brazil, for example. And any switch we have control of down there, we pick up her number and we dual route it back to NSA, a recording.

"So you don't have to be there: This says they own the network. And this is how they monitor. Now, they've got hundreds of trace route programs embedded in all this stuff. And what trace route does, it allows them to trace the route of the individual packets of the transmission going through the network: You know, if your email gets broken down into say 20 packets, they can trace the 20 packets, and how they got to where they went. So they knew the routing across every segment of the network—the time it took and all of that—and they could trace it from one point to the other. And embedded in the packet is the originator ID, and the ultimate recipient ID, so you can trace everything from end to end. And even if they try to manipulate that internally in different places, you can still follow that through the switches and the servers and the networks and the implants you've got.

"So I knew that NSA wouldn't say 'we've got high confidence.' They should say 'we know who did it'—there's no question; I mean, they did that with the Chinese, a few years ago. And there's no reason not to be able to do it in any hacking attempt at all.

"So if I were running it, I would have that automated. And that's the way I do things. And so it would be automatically alerted, and no one would have to ask, and we'd say 'here's who did it—here's when they did it,' and all of that."

'Let's Monitor Everybody'

"But the objective is really—this is really the ultimate one they have. This is called the TREASUREMAP program [**Fig. 3**]. You can go on the Web and read about it if you want. The basic objective is, in that little box there, 'let's monitor everybody in the world, every minute of the day, and know where they are.'

"This is unconstitutional, of course, this is all unconstitutional: That's why, when I put it in the sworn affidavit I submitted to the Third Circuit Court of Appeals—this is a lawsuit against the NSA for their illegal, unconstitutional collection of data on U.S. citizens—I included all these slides as a way of saying I know personally about all this stuff and I'm ready to testify. And that's a sworn affidavit: I'm liable to perjury there. And NSA is trying to say, 'well, he doesn't know, he's been out of this for 15 years.' But the programs they're using are the exact ones I invented for them for them 15, 25 years ago. [laughter] And so I know exactly what those programs do and how they interrelate and everything! So I was ready to testify to that and I still am, and that's why they don't want me in court.

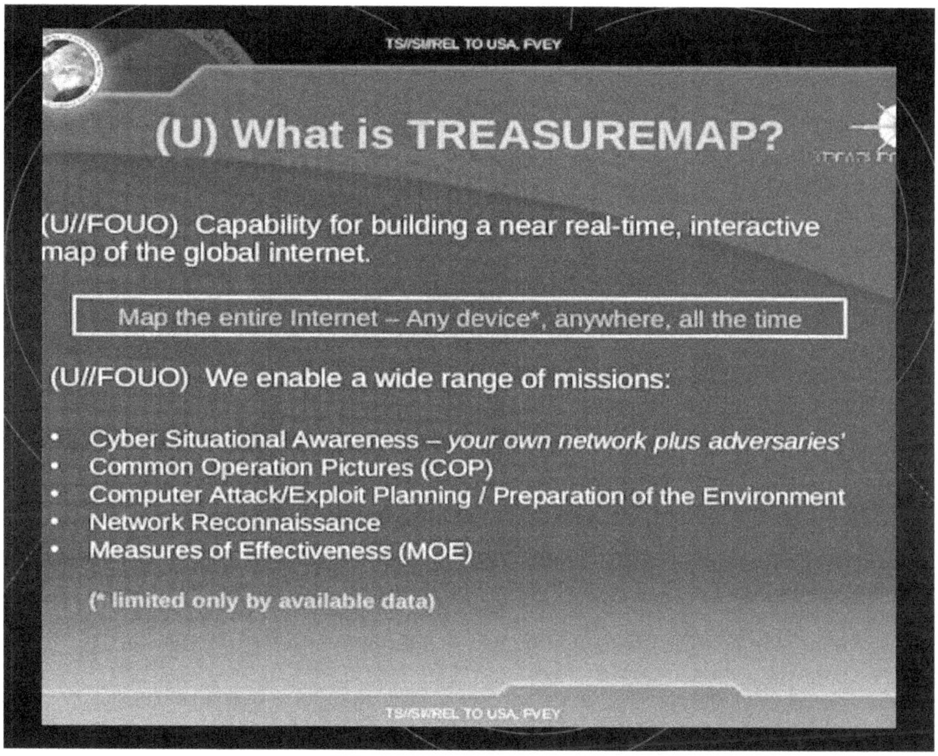

"At any rate, when it came to the Russian allegation that they did that, we started looking around; obviously I knew it was false to begin with, and I said that. But the question is, can we find some evidence of actually who did it? It took a long time before some evidence came out.

"Guccifer 2.0, I think, came out on July 5th; back then, he said, 'here's the data, and I took it out on this date.' We looked at that, and we said, 'Uh, gee, here is 1,976 MB'—a byte is eight bits apiece, so it's really about 16 gigabits of data—and [Guccifer said] 'we took it out, downloaded it over 87 seconds'; like two parts, one part initially, then a 12 minute dead time—no transmissions—and then another part came out. But overall just the transmission part was 87 seconds. So that turned out to be about 23 MB per second. And that said to me, 'Hm, that's the speed of a download through a USB port to a thumb drive, but that can't go across the worldwide network to Russia.' Because you can't get that speed for that distance."

'Bench-Marking' vs. Real-Life Hacking

Enlisting the support of those capable of doing the experiment, Binney tests the hacking hypothesis vicariously through the assistance of hacker specialists.

"Now, a lot of people said, 'Oh yeah, we can do that!' and they show it in the lab. It can go in the lab, sure, you can have a gigabit line in the lab, sure. But, let's try to get it to Russia, OK? So they kept saying, 'we'll try some more stuff in the lab.' We had a lot of tests going on—we got people testing things still, I mean, we're still looking at it. And people who are trying to do it in the lab to find some feasible way to get that rate acros—so in the meantime, I thought, why do

FIGURE 3

this in the lab, let's do it in the real world, and actually show what happens.

"So we started testing across the Atlantic to some of my hacker friends in Europe, just to say, 'Why don't you try downloading this file, close to a 1 GB, and see how fast you can get it across there?' One of our colleagues that helped write the VIPS Memo, said, 'Well, it's nice to see that the transfer rate across the Atlantic is very similar to the rate at which an iceberg melts.' [laughter] Because, we were getting it, for a 100 MB personal device at home, we were getting a transfer rate of 0.8 MB, which is about 6.4 megabits. And then, for a commercial BSO we were getting 1.6 MB, which is about one-tenth the rate we need.

"We're still testing, we're still going to do that and we're going to document our testing results. But you can't wait for the government to tell you the truth because they'll never do it. They have an agenda: Their agenda is how can we swindle you out of money, how can we keep the secret state, the shadow government running; and that's part of the point how they have to get rid of Trump, because he's not a politician, he's not from the community of government and he's a real threat to them.

"He's already talked about reorganizing the IC [in-

"Much like spotting a pig passing through a python." Binney said that any transmission of 16 gigabits across a communications network in 87 seconds, could not have been missed: "Communications networks around the world have flow monitors ... If there's any problem, they offload to other lines, reroute ... A transfer rate of 16 gigabits in 87 seconds would be very much like spotting a pig passing through a python. A network monitor would see it immediately. So we maintain that it was a local download done through a USB port."

telligence community]—which I thought I'd volunteer to help him do that! I would say, 'OK, what you have to do, see—you're fired, you're fired, you're fired, you're fired...'—you know? Clean the mess out, go down at least five levels of management, and then you might be able to start to rebuild.

"Because right now we have an intelligence community that really is a threat to our security and to our livelihood and to our safety. Because they're getting us into endless wars—I mean, Hillary Clinton even talked about sending airplanes over there to shoot down the Russian planes in Syria! C'mon! What do you want to do? create another world war, and let's start firing the missiles? Gimme a break!

"This is the agenda. That's going to cost trillions of dollars. That's what they want to do, create a new Cold War, because that's going to cost trillions of dollars—another swindle.

"So the 'fact' that we had to give up privacy to get security was a swindle; that was a lie from the very beginning. We knew how to do that, even in 1999, and they rejected it because it didn't cost a lot of money! We developed our entire program from scratch and had it deployed to three separate sites, running 24 hours a day for $3.2 million. And we were doing selected pulling of data

that was relevant, and that was all the data you got. We didn't take in any other data, so everybody had privacy as a result. And anything that we took in the metadata, we could encrypt everything; so everything you were looking at was encrypted metadata. We actually mathematically found a way of getting by the homomorphic mapping of encrypted values, which people are stumbling on right now. There's a little trick to it, but—"

Ray McGovern: "Did you have any information about 9/11?"

Binney: "Ah, yes. They had all the data to stop 9/11, before 9/11, in their databases, and didn't know it. It was all there. Even the date of the attack was given. Even the date of the attack was given! It was given in a graphic form, you know, like 9/11,—11/9 is the date. Everybody else does day/month/year; we do month/day/year—it's a progression. But at any rate, they did a line and a line, and a space; and a circle and line! 11/9. And it's the attack date, as the execution date. That was given in an email; they had that, but they didn't know it. In fact, I think according to some sources, they had actually had somebody in there who was saying the attack was coming but didn't know the date or anything, and they were trying to report that but they couldn't—NSA wouldn't let them report it.

"So we've never gotten the truth about 9/11 or many other things, and the background, the shadow government and the deep state. The companies that make all the money off all the contracts for all this crap, weapons and intelligence, manufactured one way or the other, are behind this, and that's the driving factor.

"That's what Trump is a threat to. That's why I thought he was the greatest hope we had to solve this problem, because he was an outsider, and he was at least a businessman, didn't lead in a lot of BS, in a lot of crap that was wasteful energy; and I thought that was hopeful. And since they're attacking him, I'm sure it's hopeful! [laughter] I mean, they make it obvious that they don't want him, and that's why...."

Focus on the Decision Makers— They Have Been Informed

by Adam Carter

Introduction by Jason Ross

Sept. 18—In its ongoing reporting on the fight to counter the Russia-Gate fraud being perpetrated against the U.S. Presidency, a fraud which is creating the very real threat of an unnecessary war with Russia, *EIR* is pleased to print, by permission, Adam Carter's article of Sept. 11, "Focus On The Decision-Makers—They Have Been Informed."

In his article, Carter considers the potential responses to the detailed report, "Non-Existent Foundation for Russian Hacking Charge," written by Skip Folden, a retired IT executive at IBM and a co-author of the July 24, Veteran Intelligence Professionals for Sanity (VIPS) memo addressed to President Trump, "Was the 'Russian Hack' an Inside Job?"

Adam Carter has played a major role in the investigation of the hoax which claimed that Russia hacked the DNC and made Trump President, by means of his own analysis of the online persona Guccifer 2.0, who appeared immediately after it was announced that WikiLeaks would be releasing documents related to Hillary Clinton, and just when the DNC was announcing that the firm CrowdStrike had shown their computers to have been hacked by Russian state agencies.

Adam Carter has shown that purported hacker Guccifer 2.0, who was intended to appear as a Russian trying to hide his identity by posing as a Romanian, has in reality no verifiable links either to Russia or to WikiLeaks, and that the clumsily added Russian "fingerprints" sprinkled through the documents released by Guccifer 2.0, were intended to paint with a Russian brush beforehand any documents later released by WikiLeaks that were prejudicial to the DNC and Clinton.

His work, which can be found at the website, http://g-2.space, has played an important role in bringing the truth about the hacking hoax to light. Here, he urges readers to familiarize themselves with the facts of the case, and to apply pressure to ensure that the politically motivated investigation by Robert Mueller does not lead to an unneeded and deadly war with Russia. "Without pressure," he writes, "America might never get to know the truth about what is one of the biggest public deceptions I've personally witnessed in my life, and one that I am absolutely certain of—and appalled by!" Adam Carter's article follows.

Introduction

Sept. 11—As you've probably noticed, VIPS signatories (and associates supporting the new announcements and memos) are not backing down in a hurry. Ray McGovern was recently on Redacted Tonight and *EIR* magazine just hosted an event featuring both Ray McGovern and Bill Binney, available to watch on YouTube, titled "The Russian Hack Inside Job: Who's Trying To Destroy The Presidency And Start A World War With Russia?" (Worth watching even just for Binney's explanation of the NSA's capabilities and why he is sure the NSA lacked actual evidence of a hack!)

There are good reasons these VIPS members are not backing down. Not only do they have all the information that's been brought to light over the last nine months by independent researchers, they also have direct experience of working in intelligence agencies, and Binney, alone, knows all about the NSA's capabilities because he played a fundamental role in developing the NSA's data-gathering operations.

"Most critics have chosen to ignore the mountain of circumstantial evidence gathered as well as some key pieces of verifiable evidence ..."

Critics Have *Not* Debunked the Research

The framing from most critics recently has done little more than construct a straw-man to attack (typically by making it appear as though confidence of those calling for investigation is solely based on transfer speeds that were mentioned in the 7th conclusion in Forensicator's analysis).

Most critics have chosen to ignore the mountain of circumstantial evidence gathered as well as some key pieces of verifiable evidence:

• Inconsistencies and anomalies with Guccifer 2.0's (G2's) behavior versus his stated intentions

• The consistent poor quality of G2's leaks (link)

• Predictable outcome in terms of headlines he would generate in the media (link)

• His multi-part Russian-origin deception and that GRU/FSB and allies would not purposefully draw attention to Russia (link)

• Associating self to WikiLeaks on day #1 and on various dates after that (including the day the DNC emails were published) (link)

• Creating a blog and luring in press with the Trump research (the timing of it in relation to CrowdStrike/DNC announcements and the nature of the first documents leaked) (link)

• The linguistic analysis showing no syntactical traits of a Russian communicating in English (link)

• The discredited breach claims (link)

• The fact none of his hacks were verifiable

• The premise of a talented hacker adopting another hacker's name and sticking "2.0" on the end of it

• That every association between G2 and the APT28/29 malware and infrastructure ended up collapsing under scrutiny (link)

• The attempt to fool (with multimedia props) a reporter into thinking G2 was tied to a hacker with root access to DCLeaks (link).

Critics have focused on the dissent that's come from other VIPS members, or focused on secondary sources such as the authors of articles about the VIPS memo, and their editors and publishers, rather than actually looking at the true scope of evidence involved.

Some have even tried to throw experts at this, but, as I've made clear, estimates and assumptions, even coming from experts, are no substitute for actually testing out theories and assumptions.

Recent Activities & What Will Happen Next

Since the original report was sent out, Skip Folden, one of the co-authors of the VIPS report, has sent a far more detailed report to the Office of Special Counsel (Robert Mueller), Office of the Attorney-General (as Jeff Sessions has recused himself, this has been sent to Rod J. Rosenstein, Deputy Attorney General) and, I believe more recently, to additional parties that will be disclosed in the week ahead (along with further details about the contents of that report).

The new report covers more than any of the previous reports (going beyond what Forensicator and myself even have the means to assess). While I do not have full details yet, and won't until it is published, I do know it should easily provide enough information to leave no doubt that further investigation is needed.

Update

Both the Senate and House Intelligence Committees as well as the Senate Judicial Committee, have now received [Folden's] report, all with a copy of the cover letter that was sent to Mueller and Rosenstein.

That cover letter specifically asked for (1) Verification of the report's findings, (2) Investigations resulting from the verifications, and (3) Prosecutions, as a threat to national security, of any findings of collusion to mislead or misrepresent, the results of which could not only weaken our nation through political upheaval, but risk eventual war with Russia due to the resultant downward spiral of relations.

The Odds Still Against Us—The Problems

There's no point pretending otherwise, the odds are against us. The truth getting out about the Guccifer 2.0 operation has a significant impact on various things, among them:

• The reputations of various intelligence agencies

and the programs they operate, in turn affecting budgets those agencies (and/or departments within them) are allocated.

- The reputation of various businesses in the information security industry and subsequently their stock prices and their ability to secure public sector contracts.
- The reputation of several high-profile politicians due to their probable involvement.
- The reputation of many in the mainstream media due to the propaganda they've been erroneously peddling for the last 15 months.
- The reputations of various technology & cyber-security writers that missed many things in 2016 that have since been discovered in 2017.

There are billions of dollars and the reputations of many at stake.

We have the USIC (United States Intelligence Community), mainstream media & much of the political establishment across both parties that are likely to oppose this aggressively.

We also face the prospect that Mueller will likely be resistant to putting any real pressure on Shawn Henry & Dmitri Alperovitch, especially as the former had close ties with Mueller in the past. This is fundamentally important as there are a *lot* of questions that should be asked of these particular CrowdStrike executives—and there's a good chance they will never be grilled over this.

Without pressure, America might never get to know the truth about what is one of the biggest public deceptions I've personally witnessed in my life, and one that I am absolutely certain of—and appalled by!

So, What's the Plan?

I'm just asking everyone to familiarize themselves with the facts as much as possible, to keep an eye out for the report in the week or so ahead, and look at how those who have received copies of the report (including any additional parties that are disclosed) react (or fail to).

There's a good chance they will start off by not even acknowledging receipt of the report in the hope all of this can be ignored. If we want to see a different outcome to that, it's important that as many people as possible know which decision-makers have received the report, the scope of the report and that it's important these things are investigated (which they should be at least, if the RussiaGate investigations are actually being conducted in good faith).

If you feel strongly enough about the outcome (or lack of an outcome) and want all the evidence investigated so America has a chance of finding out the truth about Guccifer 2.0, all I ask is that you speak up about how you feel and share the upcoming news far and wide.

Multiple parties now have details of the exculpatory evidence (produced throughout 2017, since the USIC wrote their assessments). This evidence far surpasses the evidence implicating Russia as far as Guccifer 2.0 is concerned, and some of it even debunks the assertions used to claim an association between Guccifer 2.0 and Russia.

VIPS, myself, and a number of researchers that have contributed to the new findings over the past year could all do with your help in making sure this information goes public, and to make sure there is pressure placed on decision-makers to investigate what has been found, to act in good faith and to *not* betray the public's trust on this even if that doesn't fit nicely with what they have told us so far!

To all who are willing to get the word out and put pressure on those that need encouragement to investigate things thoroughly——please know, in advance, that I'm extremely grateful for your help and support.

If you have any questions or concerns, I'm only an email away (see: home page).

Clarifications:

An initial version of this article had stated:

Office of the Attorney-General (Jeff Sessions).

This was changed to: Office of the Attorney-General (as Jeff Sessions has recused himself, this has been sent to Rod J. Rosenstein, Deputy Attorney General).

WHEN TRAGEDY CREATES OPPORTUNITY

Time Is Ripe for a Capital Budget For the United States

by Harley Schlanger

Sept. 15—According to the major American media, the first eight months of the Trump Presidency have been a total disaster, characterized by dysfunction and chaos in the Executive Branch, which their reporters and editorial writers attribute to the President's personality, his arrogance, ignorance, incompetence, inexperience, etc.

They point to no significant legislative victories, a worsening of relations with Russia, the threat of attack from a nuclear-armed North Korea, and increasing polarization among elected officials and within the general public, to argue that he should be removed from office, either by impeachment or by the 25th Amendment—which allows for the President to be removed for physical or mental incompetence—before he plunges the nation into civil or nuclear war.

The same media responsible for this narrative have been cheerleading what the President has accurately called the "witchhunt" against him run by former Director of the FBI and now Special Counsel Robert Mueller, who is investigating the *fraudulent* charges that Trump's election victory was based on Russian meddling and Trump's "collusion" with Russia's President Putin. Mueller is acting in coordination with what is referred to as the "Deep State"—i.e., the British intelligence networks, Obama holdovers, and corrupt officials of both parties—which is intent on blocking Trump from breaking with the endless wars and endless bailout policies of his two predecessors.

The failure to find even a scrap of evidence to prove their allegations has not diminished the howling of the media hyenas, who wish to pull off a regime-change coup in the United States. Irrefutable evidence that Americans are tired of the constant harangues about *an alleged* threat from Moscow, and that Trump's supporters still support him, have driven the anti-Trump forces into ever more hysterical attacks.

All these pundits miss the irony: their obsessive coverage of every leak coming from London and U.S. intelligence officials against Trump, has played a major role in preventing him from concentrating on fulfilling the promises he made during his successful election campaign, as he has been forced to expend time and energy in fending off these charges. While he has made significant progress in coordinating with Russian President Putin to defeat the terrorists and end the regime-change war against President Assad's government in Syria, despite the attacks in the media and by the Congress against Russia, and despite Trump's establishing a cooperative relationship with China's President Xi Jinping—both of which have

Xinhua/Ting Shen

Former FBI Director Robert Mueller (front), the special counsel probing Russian interference in the 2016 U.S. election, after meeting with the Senate Judiciary Committee, June 21, 2017.

President Trump meeting with (on the far right) Senator Chuck Schumer and Congresswoman Nancy Pelosi, Sept. 6, 2017.

been ignored or downplayed by the media—his domestic agenda is stalled.

His promise to repeal Obamacare was undermined by his supposed Republican allies, and his efforts to build modern American infrastructure have yet to begin, largely due to sabotage by Wall Street operators in his administration, such as Treasury Secretary Steven Mnuchin, by "fiscal conservatives" among Republicans, and by Democrats tied to Obama and Hillary Clinton, who refuse to accept that they lost the 2016 election.

Add to this picture the threat of a government default if the debt ceiling is not raised in September and two Category 4 hurricanes hitting the United States in successive weeks, and the potential for tragedy is great.

Debt Limit Deal

It was in the midst of the horrific destruction unleashed by Hurricane Harvey, largely as a result of the failure to follow through on necessary water management and flood control projects which had been mapped out for years for the Houston, Texas area, that Trump saw an opening to move on the economy. As U.S. deficit spending has gone up every year during the George W. Bush and Obama presidencies, there has been an increasingly partisan and nasty annual battle over raising the debt limit, to avoid a default on outstanding government debt.

The debt limit is the total amount of money that the United States is authorized to borrow to meet its existing legal obligations, including Social Security, Medicare benefits, military salaries, interest on the national debt, tax refunds, and other payments. The debt limit does not authorize new spending commitments; it simply allows the government to finance existing obligations that Congresses and Presidents have made in the past.

First enacted in 1917, Congresses and Presidents have raised the debt ceiling more than 110 times, often following threats of government shutdown from both parties. In recent years, under the influence of Wall Street-funded neo-liberal think tanks, "deficit hawks" in Congress have stubbornly insisted that they would vote to raise the debt limit only if major budget cuts were implemented.

It is these neo-liberal think tanks which have shaped the current economic/financial policy matrix, based on reducing the powers of the federal government, particularly the authority to regulate banking, finance, and insurance, and in support of "free trade" deals, which have been a major part of the outsourcing of manufacturing that has devastated industrial production and the skilled labor force over the last three decades.

As this year's deadline approached, the question was: Would Republican deficit hawks, the ideological proponents of neo-liberal economics, force a government shutdown, by refusing to raise the limit if the Democrats did not agree to the significant spending cuts the hawks were demanding?

With the anti-Trump media relishing the thought that the standoff would lead minimally to a government shutdown, if not to the first ever U.S. Treasury default— which would occur under Trump, who they then would hold responsible for what would likely trigger a global financial crisis—he pulled the rug out from under them, making a deal with Democratic leaders Chuck Schumer in the Senate and Nancy Pelosi in the House. The deal is not only to raise the debt ceiling for three months, but to add over $15 billion in spending in aid to victims of Hurricane Harvey. Acting over the heads of his party leaders, McConnell and Ryan, and his Treasury Secretary Mnuchin, President Trump has provoked the wrath of both the party leaders and the fiscal hawks.

Trump went further, saying he had spoken with Schumer about the possibility of eliminating the debt limit altogether, adding on Sept. 7, that "There are a lot

A tunnel will be built under the West Side Yard in Manhattan (shown here) to avoid a potential conflict between the Gateway Project and the Hudson Yards project.

of good reasons for doing that." Dumping the debt limit could be part of an entire rethinking of debt and deficit spending, and would be a necessary factor in a move away from the neo-liberal orthodoxy controlling both parties, opening the door to the revival of a system of Hamiltonian credit, to fund the real productive capability of the U.S. economy. The increase in real value in the economy resulting from such a change, would replace fixation over deficits, with investments to revive the growth of the real economy. The subsequent move away from the financial debt system of private central banks, would allow credit to be created directly for productive investments and not for promoting speculative bubbles.

Trump is well aware that many of the Republican members of Congress do not support his economic agenda, as they are beholden to the Wall Street financial swindlers who demanded the repeal of Glass-Steagall and the free trade deals Trump has been opposing. He is also aware that they have no legitimate policy orientation of their own, and that support for Republican Congressional leadership has dropped among Republican voters from 75% last January, to 39% today. Trump added to their dismay when he met with sixteen state and Federal elected officials from New York and New Jersey, from both parties on Sept. 7, to push ahead the Gateway Project for rebuilding transportation infrastructure for those two states. As a result, an initial government commitment of $906 million for the project passed the Congress by a 260 to 159 vote, with bipartisan support. This will begin moving on what will ultimately require between $13 billion to $15 billion to

complete. It could be the start of a multi-trillion dollar investment plan, to rebuild American infrastructure, with bipartisan support.

While Republican leaders are hysterical over what they privately are calling a betrayal, some Democrats are realizing that they must work with Trump, if only to avoid a collapse of their own party. Senator Diane Feinstein shocked supporters in San Francisco last week when she rejected calls to impeach Trump, saying that, if Trump can learn and change, "he can be a good president." Perhaps she understands that as long as the Democratic Party remains tethered to anti-Trump Republicans and Deep State anti-Russia fanatics pursuing regime change, it will continue its decline.

In his opening remarks to a meeting of Congressmen from both parties on Sept. 13, Trump said of bipartisan activity, "That's a positive thing, and it's good for the Republicans and good for the Democrats. And this group knows that very well. Whether we can do the incredible things that we're doing—and working in a bipartisan fashion, obviously, would be a positive and, I think, something . . . that we all feel good about."

As Americans from all over the country are pitching in to rebuild after the results of Hurricanes Harvey and Irma, Trump added, "Inspired by the example of our own citizens, we should be able to come together to make government work for the people—that's why I was elected, that's why I ran—and to provide jobs and opportunities to millions of struggling families." He added that, in addition to tax reform, infrastructure investments are "urgently needed... For decades now, Washington has allowed our infrastructure to fall into a state of total decay and disrepair. And it's time now to build new roads, new bridges, airports, tunnels, highways, and railways all across our great land." When differences are put aside, "We put our country and we put the citizens of our country first. And that's what this is all about."

Capital Budget

And what should be the subject of bipartisan cooperation?

The answer was provided by American economist Lyndon LaRouche in two papers he wrote in 2006-07, on why it is essential to adopt the concept of a "Capital Budget." At a time when virtually all economists were hailing the growth of the speculative bubble in mortgage-backed securities and trading in derivatives as if they were real, sustained growth, LaRouche persistently warned that this was actually accelerating the collapse of the physical economy and would bankrupt the financial system. In the Jan. 27, 2006 issue of *Executive Intelligence Review,* under the title "Deficits As Capital Gains: How to Capitalize a Recovery," LaRouche presented a compelling case for setting up a separate Federal Capital Budget to fund a massive infrastructure program. By

cc/Ray Devlin

The Surge Barrier built by the U.S. Army Corps of Engineers in New Orleans, begun in 2008 and costing $1.1 billion.

separating the credit for this from the budget of federal government operating costs, federal credit would be made available for funding infrastructure.

This is the principle of Hamiltonian credit, which is an essential feature of LaRouche's *Four Laws,* which he drafted in June 2014. Adopting this approach would lead to productive job creation and increased productivity from the application of new technologies. The result: real, physical economic growth and the creation of real, physical wealth, instead of bubbles.

LaRouche developed this further, in an article published in *EIR* on Jan. 12, 2007 titled "The Lost Art of the Capital Budget." In this article, LaRouche exposed the axiomatic flaws in the neo-liberal austerity regimes, which still dominate economic thinking in the trans-Atlantic world. The neo-liberal cant, of counting "every budgeted dollar of public expenditures as outlays which must be balanced by current tax receipts," ensures that there will be no investment in future physical progress. To argue, as the neo-liberals do, that sound financial policy places today's "bottom line" profits ahead of necessary investments for the future, represents a rejection of the American System of physical economy, in favor of the Anglo-Dutch liberal system.

As an example of this, LaRouche pointed to the idiocy of the state of Louisiana in rejecting repairs to the antiquated water management and flood control system protecting New Orleans, as "too expensive," choosing instead to offer subsidies to build casinos. When Hurricane Katrina hit in August 2005, the city was unprepared, resulting in more than 1,800 deaths. For a small percentage of the estimated $200-plus billion in economic losses suffered by the city and state, the infrastructure could have been brought up to modern standards, saving lives and money.

Applying the Hamiltonian credit system advocated by LaRouche would "promote the reinvestment of retained earnings (i.e., 'profit') in the form of technologically physical advancements of products and productivity." As Hamilton's policies did, in the first years of the U.S. republic, debt would be turned into the basis of investment, to produce more value than what is required to retire the debt! By implementing a Capital Budget system, there would never again be a problem with a debt limit, as this would allow for a full transformation of the U.S. economy, from a monetary system run by, and for, powerful speculative financial interests, to a physical economy, whose growth would benefit every citizen.

Out of the destructive tragedy of the two recent hurricanes, and the disruption caused by the attempted overthrow of the Trump Presidency, the potential has now emerged to take up the challenge of reviving Hamilton's system, something which the President has said he wants to do. Now is the time for President Trump to organize bipartisan support for LaRouche's Four Laws, with the implied element of a Capital Budget as part of a Hamiltonian credit system. With presidential leadership for this program, the attempt at a regime change coup would be crushed.

How Could LaRouche Forecast This Just Five Years Ago?

In the LaRouche PAC Friday webcast of Sept. 15, excerpted below, host Matthew Ogden showed that Lyndon LaRouche had forecast the unexpected U.S. political developments of the past few days, exactly five years ago, on the occasion of his 90th birthday, 2012.

Matthew Ogden: Now, what we're going to do for our broadcast tonight, is actually rewind a few years. We're going to roll back history about five years, and we're going to go back to Mr. Lyndon LaRouche's 90th birthday. On that occasion, Mr. LaRouche delivered what has now become a fairly famous speech in which he called for the end of the party system; but he also lays out the program for the economic recovery of the United States, and a completely new vision for what has to happen in terms of international relations and the policy of this country.

A lot has happened since that time, five years ago. It almost seems like an eternity ago in terms of the course of world history. If you think about what has occurred, this speech you're about to see a part of, was given before the Chinese adoption of the New Silk Road as their official policy—the Belt and Road Initiative; before the plethora of new development banks that came out of the BRICS countries—the New Development Bank and the Asia Infrastructure Investment Bank; before all of these developments that happened abroad. And of course, before the watershed election of 2016 that happened here in the United States.

If you look at what has happened in the United States, granted this speech that you're about to see a part of, was given during the 2012 Presidential elections that were a contest between Barack Obama and Mitt Romney, if you can remember. But it's almost phenomenal how prescient Mr. LaRouche was, for what was about to occur in the United States, something that nobody else saw coming, and probably were in disbelief when they listened to the words that Lyndon LaRouche said at that time. If you think about both so-called political parties in this previous Presidential election, both of them ceased to exist in their previous form. There's no recognizable Democratic Party, nor recognizable Republican Party. Perhaps some of the same personalities are still there, but the so-called establishment parties that we had before 2016, before the insurgency in the Democratic Party that took form around Bernie Sanders, and then the insurgency in the Republican Party that took form around Donald Trump; before both of those happened, Mr. LaRouche was laying out what he called the end of the establishment party system which was destroying the very soul of the United States.

We've seen that going into the 2016 elections, and we said this very clearly, there was much more that unified the American people, that united the American people than divided the American people. Look at the broad support for Glass-Steagall for example; something you're about to hear Mr. LaRouche talk about in this speech from five years ago. Look at the broad support for infrastructure, for productive jobs; look at the broad opposition to the confrontation with Russia that was going to lead to World War III. This is what Hillary Clinton's campaign represented in the eyes of the American people. This is what the establishment Republicans' various campaigns represented in the eyes of the American people. There was much more at that time that unified the American people than divided the American people. In fact, it was the LaRouche program.

But, if you come to the present day and think about what has happened in the United States just over the past few weeks, we can see again that the American people are becoming united. Look at what happened in Houston around the recovery in Harvey; the kind of selflessness and love for their fellow man that everybody showed in terms of this effort to go out to save and protect people from this natural disaster. This recognized no divisions; there were no party lines. There was no "Are you a majority, are you a minority? Are you a Republican, are you a Democrat? Are you a conservative, are you a liberal?" Everybody was an American. The same sentiment happened in Florida in the wake of Hurricane Irma there. Now we can see this even spilling over into politics in Washington. In a very nascent form, but the President of the United States has now very much offended his Republican Party establishment figures—the Mitch McConnells and the Paul Ryans—by reaching out to the Democratic Party to put through a recovery program for Houston and to start working on some of the policy that should have been policy from Day One. This was supposed to be the first 100 days of this Presidency: infrastructure; productive jobs. This is now beginning to emerge finally in its nascent form; and it's our responsibility to continue to lead.

Lyndon LaRouche at his 90th birthday party, Sept. 9, 2012.

But what I want to do is play this excerpt from Mr. LaRouche's remarks. I think you'll find it fascinating, reflecting on what has happened in the past five years between Mr. LaRouche's 90th birthday and Mr. LaRouche's 95th birthday. In fact, what is the power of ideas to shape history? What do we have to expect in the days, weeks, months, and years to come? This is the vision of that leadership, that statesman-like leadership that you're about to hear from Mr. LaRouche. This is how history is formed.

[Video excerpt begins.]

Lyndon LaRouche: The problem is, *the party system.*

Now, George Washington, President George Washington and others, at the founding of our republic, as an independent republic, tried to *prevent* the formation of *a party system.* And I think, the time has come, to eliminate *the party system.* [applause] At this time, it's the only way, formally, through the legal process, that we could eliminate the possibility of these two kinds of Presidents.

What's wrong? Why should we have *party systems*? We have a Constitution, which is defined; the Constitution is fine, if it's carried through, as intended; it is our system. But why do we have to have parties intervening in between the process of selecting Presidential leadership in national government? Why do we do that? What screwball invented this kind of nonsense? Because that's what happened: People become partisan, and say, "which party wins is going to determine the fate of the nation!"

No party has that kind of right! There can not be a party, that has the right, to oversee and control the destiny of the nation! You can have a President, there's nothing wrong with that. But you can't have a President as the President of a party. Or, you can not have a conniving, between two Presidential teams, or two party teams, which connive by special agreement among themselves, to create the composition of a national government! These things are obscenities, which leaders of our nation, beginning from the George Washington Administration, recognized as evils! And the idea of going to a European kind of government, which is inherently corrupt—by its very nature, not necessarily by the *intention* of the people, or the intention of the politicians, *they just don't know any better!*

And the only way this can be done, is, if we infect the population, with the realization, *we do not want a party system!* We have state governments, don't we? Under our Constitution. We have local governments, within state governments, under our Constitution. We have bodies which the nation creates, to perform functions of the Federal government, the military and the rest of it. *So we don't need parties!* They don't do any damned good!

I mean, it's like Franklin Roosevelt: If Franklin Roosevelt had just been the President and didn't have to deal with these damned parties, we would not have had the mess we got into. What we need, we need to have *not* a contention, over which *party* is going to win, when the party was *not]* inherent in the conception of nation. *What we need is a Federal Republic, with its state composition and other local compositions playing their role.*

We don't need this party system which is a system of inherent corruption. What we need, is the election, due process election, of a composition of government. And we don't want people diverting the attention of the population, from the issues of the nation, over the issues of partisanship! *That's* where the problem lies!

When you rely on parties, as such, you set up a kind of controversy, or competition, for power, between or among party systems. These party systems then *excite the passions* of the foolish voters, who now are concerned about voting for the *party, first,* and the *nation, second!* When it must be the *nation, first,* and not the party.

The Basis of Corruption

The voluntary part of the system, that's fine; the citizen has a right, to make formations, to make agreements among themselves, and to cast their votes accordingly, and to discuss these matters accordingly. But we don't want the top-down rule of a party system, which is controlled by the money sent to them, by financial interests which control the money which gives one party advantage over the other! You want the bare citizen, as a citizen, to have an equal right, and independence of this party system.

This has been said, again and again, in the course of the history of the United States! That people with insight, realize that the essence of the corruption in the United States, is based in and derived from the use of the party system. And you see it right now: You have, the nation is now mortgaged, for the selection of its government, its national government, is mortgaged to the *party system!* Everything is stopped, except which party is going to win! And one is almost as bad as the other.

And why should we be spending our time, selecting a government, of two parties, neither of which is fit to be our government! Why don't we have a national government selected in the way that George Washington, for example, President George Washington, had intended? We would not *have* that mess! And the citizen would be called upon, not to decide who's butt he wants to kiss, but rather what the issues are and programs that this citizen wishes to express. We want to engage the citizen in the dialogue! We don't want to take the competition *between* groups of citizens. *We want the citizen to force the reality, that he or she is voting for the government.* And what the citizens do in voting for a government, will determine the fate of the nation.

We want to *confront* the citizen, with the responsibility of *his* being accountable, or her being accountable, for the responsibility of what government is, and what it becomes. We have to *force* responsibility upon the individual citizen, as a citizen, not as a sucker, playing into some kind of game. And this has been understood for a long time, by the best thinkers of the United States, that

it is the party system, as typified by the Andrew Jackson Presidency, one of the most corrupt Presidencies in our history. And the corruption that was done, to the United States, by the election of Andrew Jackson, and the people who controlled him, which were British bankers; so, Andrew Jackson was a tool of British imperial bankers: They owned him. They ran him. And it was because of the party system, that this could happen.

And we got the same thing today: You're shacked up with a couple of clowns—Dummo and the Crook, and the Insane Crook.

Now, the only thing we can do, or the only thing I can do, on this thing right now, apart from telling you this wonderful information, is to awaken you to realize what we're really up against, to recognize what the real problems are. If you're thinking about looking at this mess out there, from the standpoint of Democratic or Republican, you're not thinking! Because you're not thinking in terms of the essential interest. Because what you're doing, whatever you do, you are imprisoned to pledging your support, to a party! Not to the nation. Yes, you say, "to the nation," but it's the party that controls you. And that is how Andrew Jackson destroyed the United States, it was with the party system! That's what doomed Franklin Roosevelt. Franklin Roosevelt would never have had this clown, Truman, stuck on him, except for the party system business. And that's where our problem lies.

And we have to make that clear. Because we know what the state of mind is. What's the state of mind of the voter? He's playing football, not politics! He's playing a version of football, baseball, whatever—gambling! Racketeering, whatever! And his mind, his passion, is associated with winning this, for this party, this team, this, that, that, and so forth—*not for the nation!* The objective of our system of government must be to *force the citizen, as a citizen, to think through what the national interest is!* And we don't do it. We say, "Which party are you going to support?" Well, what's the party going to do? "Well, I think it's a good party," in other words, they don't know what the hell they're doing—and their passion is involved in being sure they won't know it. And that's where we stand. And that's the thing we've got to think about.

And you've got to destroy the self-confidence of

those damned fools, who think that the "party vote," the vote for the party *should determine the decision of the nation.* That is a false and fraudulent conception, and it's about time we called a halt to it. And right now, would be a very good time. All right. [applause]

Now, what're we going to do? Let's lay out, here, we have our organization. We have a conception of how to organize this nation, how to deal with the great crisis, the financial crisis, the economic crises, which occur in this nation; and which occur, also, similarly, in other nations, which I think would tend, at this time, to look with a friendly eye at what I might propose here, right now.

All right: First of all, the world is bankrupt. The trans-Atlantic region is *totally, hopelessly bankrupt!* Every part of Western and Central Europe is totally bankrupt! It's *incurably* bankrupt, under its present system. Nothing be done to save it in its present form. There's no way you can bail it out! There's no way you can take it out of this—except one way: Glass-Steagall.

Now, of late, you will have observed that Glass-Steagall has become increasingly popular, in England, in the continent of Europe, and other notable places! So what does Glass-Steagall do? Well, essentially it says that the system of government we're running under right now, is hopelessly corrupt; so, let's shut it down! Let's shut down all the bailouts. We're not going to pay it! We jes' ain't gonna pay it! [applause]

So what're we going to do? Well, we're going to have a grand old time: We're going to go to a straight credit system, which is Glass-Steagall, immediately! Now, that means, that all those other guys, the gamblers, Wall Street types and so forth, are going to find themselves sitting—well: They have all these claims. All these values. They own all this property, in terms of title. But we say, the point is here, with Glass-Steagall, that you can run your kind of banking system if you want to—under penalties of law, of course! But you don't have any right to come to the Federal government, to demand that the Federal government bail them out, if they happen to go bankrupt.

Now, I can tell you, as you probably have suspected, that practically every part of the whole system in the United States, today, *is already hopelessly, incurably bankrupt!* And there's only one way we can escape from this bankruptcy: You want to have some money to live on? There's one thing you got to do: Glass-Steagall! And that will open the… it won't solve the problem, but it will open the gates, to permit the problem to be solved.

If you take, and say, all these things that are not and don't conform to Glass-Steagall, all these things must be cancelled. That means these banks can still have their banking system, as long as they don't go bankrupt. We're not going to shut them down arbitrarily, we're just letting them out on their own, and saying, "this is not our business. The Federal government is not responsible for this."

All right, now that will reduce the debt of the United States, *tremendously!* It would have a similar effect in nations of Europe! The French banks would not be pleased with me. They would probably say some very nasty things about me, but… things like that.

But the point is, the world now knows, and increasingly in Europe, and starting in England and other countries in Europe itself, there's an understanding that Glass-Steagall is a necessary alternative. And these guys are having a terrible time, in fighting off the Glass-Steagall popularity. But that will do it.

The problem is, because we waited so long, since we cancelled Glass-Steagall, we waited too long, and they ran up a hyperinflationary debt, which is really beyond even dreaming. So therefore, the result is, if we go with Glass-Steagall, we're going to have relatively little money, under our Federal system; because we wasted it by throwing it into the garbage pail, and we can't get it back. So therefore, we're going to have to go to another measure. Now, I said, national banking. Now, why national banking? Because, unless you create a banking system, under the U.S. government, under protection and regulation of the U.S. government, you can't do anything much with the economy.

Where Will the Money Come From?

We have very little industry left in the United States, it's been systematically destroyed. Especially since the last three terms of the Presidency. We have been running a garbage pail; and therefore, we have no means, by ordinary means, to save the economy. We don't have jobs. Now, as most of you know, under NAWAPA [the North American Water and Power Alliance], we would create, quickly, *4 million or more jobs*—real jobs! Really productive jobs. We would create, at least, immediately, a couple million more highly skilled categories of jobs. We would start the process of a general recovery of the United States—but oh! Wait a minute! Got one more problem. Where's the money going to come from, that we're going to loan, for NAWAPA, and loan for other high-technology jobs, and certain other kinds of skilled jobs? The Federal government is going to have to *create credit*, which will be run through a national banking system, so that under national banking and Federal government approval, we can conduit credit into creating these jobs.

Let's take the practical question of the food supply in the United States right now: As you probably know, food is about to be cancelled, and the Obama Administration is doing everything possible to destroy it. Because they're doing everything to destroy food, for fuels.

So therefore, what're we going to do? Well, what we're going to do, is by giving the Federal credit, into, say, the NAWAPA system, we're going to create a flow of credit, into the various phases of this process, which will immediately charge NAWAPA, in particular, and other things that go with NAWAPA. We have also, we have the lost auto industry, the whole Detroit system, for example, and we're going to put that back into work! So, we're going to create, instantly, that is, by Federal decree—instantly create sufficient growth, not only to get rid of this hopeless debt, which never was really a legitimate debt, at all, and we're going to restart the economy, by taking people, when you have very few people who are actually involved in productive jobs, they're not involved in producing things; they're mostly employed in various kinds of services, which are not particularly productive, and do not lend any productive value to the U.S. economy. They're simply pass-outs, under one guise or the other.

So in this case, we are launching a recovery of the U.S. economy, by supplying credit, as we did in the beginning of the development of our economy, after we won our Revolution, we're going back to that system of recovery to get things moving, and it's going to start immediately. And the easiest way for us to do this, is NAWAPA. NAWAPA is a project, which is relevant, because it's focused on *water management*. And the problem we have in the United States today, is a water management problem! In the Central States, we don't have rain! We don't have the means to grow crops. And we don't have people who are employed, in actually productive forms of employment! Physically productive forms of employment.

The difference is, with this kind of reform, of three steps: NAWAPA as a driver, an incentive driver, which will save the organization of production in the Central and Western States of the United States! The going back into the area of the so-called Detroit area, with several million jobs, immediately, will have a similar effect. Which means that we then can use a credit system, managed under Federal control, as we've used credit systems, like Franklin Roosevelt did in the past, and use that kind of credit system under a Glass-Stea-gall type government system, and we can start the re-growth of the U.S. economy.

We also have, as a byproduct of this: If we as the United States *do* this, you will find that the nations of Eurasia, will join us. You will find that nations of Europe, who are now being destroyed by their own system, will now go back into functioning, and we will use international credit, which is an extension of the national banking concept, instead of speculation, in order to restart the economy. And that can be done.

So there is a practical solution, a *sane* practical solution, as opposed to the other kind, for this problem we have as a nation. How far are we from getting it, is the question?

Well, that depends. It depends how desperate people are, and how much their desperation is moderated by the sense of attachment to a solution. Our job is to present the solutions. You know, society is actually led, when it's led, by a tiny minority of the human race. We have not, because of our underdevelopment, we have not built up nation systems, which are actually rational, and truly represent *the will of human beings.* What we approach is the conditional will of human beings, by providing them with promises, which we hopefully can keep, and that they will be satisfied by trusting us, by the means of the measures we offer to them, as suggestions.

A very tiny minority, of the human population in all nations, actually has any comprehension, any qualifications for comprehension of how an economy runs or how it should be run. We have to bring them to us, to our ideas, our conceptions, based on the fact that they need precisely the solutions that we present. It may not be exactly what they would dream for, but it's what we could deliver! And if people understand that that's what the game is, they'll accept it, at least in large part.

It's what they can believe that we can deliver. And it's our saying that we can deliver *this,* but we *can't do* that, *yet.* And if you promise everything, they're not going to trust you, and for good reason. If you give specific promises, that *will work,* and make sense, and can be explained to the people, it'll work! And if they don't accept it, that's their fault!

But our responsibility, which is limited—we don't run the world; we don't have powers to supervise the world as a whole. We can only argue! We can only argue as an intelligentsia, that we have done some thinking that the other people have not yet caught onto, or didn't know about. And we can tell them, what *we* can do! What *we* understand, what *will* work for them; and say, "We're going to have to work harder, and better, in order to fulfill the kind of promises we wish to deliver." And say, we need their cooperation in doing that.

We've got to give them a sense, that whatever we're promising them, we're committed to delivering, and that our promise of delivery has been made credible to them. And that experience, as in the case of the Franklin Roosevelt recovery in the United States during the 1930s, the same program, the same policy that Franklin Roosevelt used in reviving the U.S. economy.

But we have to tell these guys, "Stop being the kind of idiot, who believes in the party system! That's number one. Number two, don't believe in Obama, get him out of there, and make sure he's removed quickly." And we're going to have to figure out what we're going to do about this Republican. [laughter] Because that's a real weak point, there.

However, I believe this: If we can establish a functional Presidency of the United States as was done in establishing the United States under George Washington's Presidency, if we have a President, and we use our system of government, our constitutional system of government, we can solve this problem. Not the way people would like, by "wish factory" or something, but by the fact, we can point the direction, and it's up to the people to follow the direction, and choose to follow the direction.

But we must do what is not done right now: The problem with government now, is that the U.S. government and its functions, are chiefly one, big, damned lie! They promise things that do not exist, or will not exist, and make rules which make no sense, and are willing to get into wars, by which civilization and mankind in general, could be destroyed. And we have to use that argument and that bill of particulars, as a method of convincing them, this has to be done.

And the key thing is this, to come back to the theme I started with: Space. It's obvious, there's a limited timeframe within which mankind can continue to live safely under the system of the Sun, the current Sun system. The Sun has a limited—some people say 2 billion years; some would say, well, long before 2 billion years, the Sun is going to act up, and life is going to be *most unpleasant* on this planet!

So, we as mankind, have to address this question. And it's obvious that to address this question, we have

> **We've got to give them a sense, that whatever we're promising them, we're committed to delivering, and that our promise of delivery has been made credible to them. And that experience, as in the case of the Franklin Roosevelt recovery in the United States during the 1930s, the same program, the same policy that Franklin Roosevelt used in reviving the U.S. economy.**

to give new attention, to space, the questions of space. We have to find ways of intervening in the space system, or the Solar space system and so forth, and this is possible. But we must turn to that direction, to think, "well, we can't stand around, following a fixed recipe, like a kitchen cookbook recipe, forever. We have to anticipate the problems which face mankind in the future, we have to search for solutions to those problems, and we've got to convince people.

And the big thing you have to do, is this: Most people in the United States today, behave stupidly, and this, of course, is helped by the educational system, it's helped by the terrible conditions of life of children, as well as adolescents, and there are many things that have to be done. And our job is, as a minority in society, and with other minorities in society which *wish* to find and initiate true solutions for these problems, we have to get out, and convince people, and educate them.

And in particular, get them immediately to understand, that these two Presidencies that they've stuck out there for voting, ain't shucks! And we've got to do something about that, and the best way, is to go out and say that these guys aren't fit to run anything, and give some indications of what we're thinking.

It can work. It can work because the situation of all humanity, on this planet right now, is almost a hopeless one. The war danger, the thermonuclear war which is hanging over us right now, is threat number one. The shortage of food in the United States, for people, citizens of the United States, is another. The conditions of health care, are another. All of these conditions are intolerable! *And nobody's doing a damned thing about it, from the standpoint of government on down!* I don't hear of any big riots coming out of the Congress, against the lack of such needed reforms! They're going by… the party system. And I think we have to just treat the party system, as the kind of fraud that it has always been!

We should have a system of representative government, in which the citizens can use those other citizens who are the most qualified, and the most committed, to provide leadership, to provide the ideas and the leadership which is needed for the rest. If you can't be something, inspire it in somebody else.

Thank you. [ovation]

The Simultaneity of Eternity Comes To Celebrate Lyndon LaRouche's 95th Birthday

by Michelle Rasmussen

Sept. 17—Few people reach the age of 95. That accomplishment alone is certainly cause for celebration. Fewer still have used the years they were given, long or short, to change history in the way Lyndon LaRouche has done, and to inspire so many to act to change history themselves. Therefore, during the celebration yesterday in Germany, at a wine grower's restaurant in Rheinland-Pfalz, gifts embodying the expression of human creativity were given to a man who has fought so hard, and so long, to bring the principle of human creativity into economics, into politics, into art and science, to the young and old around the world. From poetry to drama; from *lieder* and operatic arias, to choral works.

Some of Lyn's best friends from the simultaneity of eternity made special guest appearances to add to the festivities: Bach, Haydn, Beethoven, Schubert, Brahms, and Verdi, and, oh yes, Schiller, too. There was also an original poem by Helga Zepp-LaRouche, in German, and musical compositions and arrangements by some of the members of LaRouche's political movement who were present. Artistic works in German, English, Italian and Danish, and works in Chinese, Korean, and in African languages.

Words of thanks were offered to a man who has changed all of our lives—who has given us direction, purpose, and a mission on behalf of all mankind. Who has politically fought with his mind, as boxers fight

Lyndon LaRouche at his 95th birthday party with his wife Helga Zepp-LaRouche, Sept. 9, 2017.

with their fists, thus leading the way.

The participants had traveled from throughout Germany, and from France, Sweden, Denmark, the United States, and Russia, with Italy also represented. Would that we all could have been there.

Many of those who could not be present, had written contributions for a *Festschrift* (commemorative book), presented to Lyn by his wife and closest collaborator, Helga. After glasses of *Sekt* were raised to Lyn, she was coaxed into reciting the poem she had written to her dear husband, the first entry in the *Festschrift*.

The first musical offering came from John Sigerson

and Margaret Greenspan from Manhattan, with a performance of Beethoven's song-cycle *An die ferne Geliebte* (To the Distant Belovéd) which Lyn thoroughly enjoyed. That created a wonderful atmosphere for the rest of the evening. (They had traveled from the United States to sing and play for Lyn, in addition to giving two concerts in connection with the current *BüSo* election campaign run by the German section of the LaRouche movement.)

After coffee and cakes, the program resumed. Elliot Greenspan, a leader of Lyn's Manhattan Project, presented Lyn with several mementos from that Project: a picture of the New York organizers, an original drawing of Leibniz in front of the World Land-Bridge, a calendar with pictures of Manhattan Project activities, and a poem written by one of the members there. He asked Lyn if, when he initiated the Project, he had foreseen that New York City would produce the next president, Trump. Lyn responded that we don't know how far Trump will go. We need him now, but if he fails, that's his fault, and that will be regrettable—but I think he can win.

Elliot assured him that we are not just going to sit around to see what happens. You said, Elliot added, that you were too old to run for President, but not too old to shape the Presidency. You gave us the Hamilton principle and the choral principle. Gave us, and exemplified, the principle of the human mind, the principle of the flank, and Schiller's idea of the patriot and the world citizen. Speaking especially on behalf of American organizers, we are eternally grateful and committed to this mission. You might say that Trump has become our Manhattan Project, or, if you really want to make America great again, "Win with Lyn." (Lyn, while he himself was being honored, then added a thought about honoring those victims and responders who died on Sept. 11, 2001 in Manhattan.)

Afterwards, Feride Istogu Gillesberg, accompanied by Werner Hartmann, sang a Chinese folksong, "The Fisherman's Song," which poignantly expressed the longing for justice which had attracted her to Lyn's campaign. She and Michelle Rasmussen, both residents of Denmark, also gave the first performance of a song that Michelle had composed for the occasion, based on a poem by Hans Christian Andersen entitled, "Song for the Scandinavian Natural Scientists' meeting on July 9, 1840," which reveals this creative artist's excitement about scientific discovery. The poem describes the great book of nature, and the universe, which man can read and get wisdom from, and through which mankind can sense God's voice.

Then Kasia Kruczkowski from Germany spoke. She had asked several people from the simultaneity of eternity about that troublemaker Lyndon LaRouche, and she recited statements by them about what the quality of genius is, as her gift to a genius of our time:

You can know a real genius by the amount of opposition he has (Jonathan Swift and Einstein); how one who is admired by others, himself knows how far he is from his goal (Beethoven); the three moral qualities of man are wisdom, compassion, and courage (Confucius); the more we know about God's works, the more we recognize them as excellent, and in conformity with our desires (Leibniz); and, finally, that the yearning for liberty and the rights of man has been planted by God in all hearts (Benjamin Franklin)—and you, Lyn have always acted like that philosopher.

LaRouche in Dialogue

Leena Malkki from Sweden sang two songs by Schubert from his *Schwanengesang* (Swan Song), *Frühlingsbotschaft* and *Ständchen*, and thanked Lyn for his inspiration. They were among the first songs she had ever performed. She also added a song "Fidelity," by Haydn.

The Wiesbaden office choir, conducted by Werner Hartmann, sang his beautiful arrangement of the Korean folksong *Arirang*, which communicated a sincere spirit of unification.

Next came the Berlin-Dresden choir conducted by Benjamin Lylloff, which sang three folk songs, *In stiller Nacht*, *Erlaube mir*, and *All' mein Gedanken*, by Johannes Brahms. They ended with Benjamin's dynamic arrangement of the song *Nkosi sikelel' iAfrika* (God Bless Africa), well-known to many Africans. This was a joyous ending of the first part of the cultural offerings.

After a buffet dinner, the second part began with a dramatic scene from Friedrich Schiller's play *Don Carlos*, between King Philip and Elisabeth, played by Hans-Peter Müller and Christa Kaiser.

Odile Mojon from France also gave us a gigue by Bach on her violin. It is always a joy to hear her play.

Then, former French presidential candidate Jacques Cheminade started to deliver a speech for that honored occasion. But the honored man, whose life has been

Former French presidential candidate Jacques Cheminade (right) in dialog with Lyndon LaRouche at the latter's 95th birthday party.

characterized by activity, not passivity, started to respond to each idea, and what ensued was transformed from a monologue, to a dialogue, to the delight of all, including Jacques.

The back and forth started when Jacques said that Lyn and Helga's vision is now becoming reality. In the ensuing discussion, Lyn said that his devotion, his life's work, was the determination that man has to act on the universe to solve problems, and that he is a warrior to defend mankind, as mankind.

Jacques said that we are celebrating a moment in the progression of the simultaneity of eternity. You have given us a pilgrimage for the cause of the future; because of what you and Helga have done, we have a chance to be part of the future.

The discussion included a huge attack against the stupidity of the current German and French political systems, and the American population. Lyn asked if mankind can understand what's wrong with it. That's the only way to solve the problems.

The only important thing is discovery in the universe, and whether it is true or false. Look at the great job China is doing. If you understand what the truth might be, you have a chance.

Jacques concluded by saying that the songs of the future do not yet have words, but the songs presented here tonight prove that we have a potential for the future. Lyn responded that you have the potential to establish relations across the world. If you can do that, you can cause the salvation of civilization.

The solution is to develop space capabilities. Jacques said that it was his space program project that caused the French elite to want to throw him into outer space. Lyn retorted: Take it as an opportunity!

Ema Reuter from the United States then gave a very moving rendition of Schubert's *Der Wanderer* with Benjamin at the piano, followed by the uplifting quartet from Beethoven's only opera Fidelio, *Mir ist so wunderbar*, with Feride as Marzeline, Leena as Leonore, Tom Gillesberg as Rocco, and John Sigerson as Jacquino, with Benjamin on piano.

Leena sang again, very dramatically performing Desdemona's "Willow Song" and "Ave Maria" from Verdi's *Otello*, as the penultimate musical finish for the evening.

The last speaker, Tom Gillesberg, the chairman of the Schiller Institute in Denmark, said that in five years, on the occasion of Lyn's 100th birthday, he hoped to be giving a speech at the opening of LaRouche Universities in many countries. We are at a time when necessity and opportunity meet. Lyn responded by saying that you have to do it, to get victory. Bring forces in Italy, and other countries, together for a common purpose. That will do it. It's absolutely necessary—or else you will lose everything. You cannot just have offices. You have to go for it fully. Go for it to win, and win for mankind.

Afterwards, John, again accompanied by Margaret, joyously sang *Das Wandern* by Schubert. At the very end, all joined in to sing the German birthday canon *Viel Glück und Viel Segen* to Lyn.

Thus, was Lyndon LaRouche's 95th birthday celebrated, together with some of his many friends and associates, both living, and from the past, with inspiring music, and words, and good food and wine. And, not to be forgotten, his little dog Holly was also there, of course, to congratulate him.

III. Stop Saudi War Crimes in Yemen

EIR STATEMENT

Enemy of the New Silk Road Paradigm: Saudi Genocide in Yemen

Sept. 16—New revelations on the role of Saudi Arabia in the 9/11 terrorist attacks on the United States pose the imperative: The ongoing Saudi genocide against Yemen must stop; the Saudi-related networks perpetrating such crimes against humanity must be brought down. Acting on this will open wide the way for the entire world, including the Mideast, to participate in the New Silk Road development drive—the Belt and Road Initiative—which is the necessary "peace through development" process needed to end the perpetual warfare in the region.

Xinhua/Hani Ali

A market destroyed in airstrikes by the Saudi-led coalition in Sana'a, July 2015.

What is required is the creation of an international investigative commission into Saudi Arabia's actions against Yemen, and a set of immediate actions. China this week indicated its support for such an investigation, and a "political" solution.

• Stop the Saudi bombing and all other attacks on Yemen.

• Stop the Saudi blockade of Yemen's ports.

• Stop all outside interference in Yemen, to allow a return to the process of negotiation that existed before the start of the bombing, to proceed to resolution of domestic differences.

• Provide immediate food, water, electric power, and sanitation, and medical, public health, and all other social relief in full.

• Provide all other humanitarian and economic aid urgently required, especially transportation, shelter, and logistics.

• Initiate stand-by preparations for international collaboration to re-build Yemen, and welcome its participation in the development drive of the Maritime Silk Road of Eurasia-Africa.

Britain has blocked every attempt at even an international investigative commission, while Britain and the United States continue to supply arms to the Saudi "Coalition" perpetrating the criminal assault. On the American side, the very same backers of Saudi crimes are working to bring down the duly elected government of President Donald Trump. In turn, these interconnect with the British sponsors of the Saudi royalty, going back to the founding of the Saudi Kingdom.

New Evidence: Bob Mueller Complicit

The new 9/11 revelations, which came out on the eve of the 16th anniversary of that attack, concern specifically evidence of direct Saudi government involvement in the 1999-2001 preparation of the aircraft attacks—including a "dry run" flight attempt in 1999. The evidence shows a pattern of cover-up by then FBI Director Robert Mueller. This is the same Bob Mueller who ran the "Get LaRouche Task Force" in the 1980s, and now leads the investigation/assault against President Donald Trump today, based on the bogus charge of Russian interference in the U.S. election.

The new, damning documentation comes in a lawsuit against Saudi Arabia filed in New York Federal District Court by a group of families of 9/11 victims. These plaintiffs have filed an amended complaint, citing FBI documents, showing that the Saudi government employed and financed two Saudi "students" in the U.S.—

Mohammed al-Qudhaeein and Hamdan al-Shalawi—whose attempts to gain access to the cockpit of an America West flight from Phoenix to Washington, D.C., in November 1999, were of such a threatening nature that the plane made an emergency landing in Ohio.

The two were arrested when the plane landed, and questioned by the FBI, but were then released. The FBI later "discovered" that the two—

• Had been trained in Afghanistan, and had regular contacts with one of the Saudi hijacker-pilots and a senior al-Qaeda leader from Saudi Arabia, now held in the Guantanamo prison,

• Were employed by the Saudi government, and

• Were in "frequent contact" with Saudi officials while in the United States, including attending a symposium hosted by the Saudi Embassy and chaired by the Saudi Ambassador. The Saudi Embassy even paid for the pair's tickets for the "dry-run" flight.

There is also new attention to the attempted cover-up by then FBI Director Robert Mueller, which puts him into the spotlight for his role against Trump today. At the time of the 2002 investigation by the Joint Congressional Inquiry into 9/11, Mueller prevented the Congressional investigators from interrogating an FBI informant, Abdussattar Shaikh, who had harbored two of the 9/11 Saudi hijackers in San Diego before the attack.

Mueller removed Shaikh to an undisclosed location so he couldn't be questioned, defying even a Congressional subpoena for his testimony. Sen. Bob Graham, co-chairman of the Joint Congressional Inquiry, thinks that Mueller acted on the authority of the White House, indicating the Bush family's alignment with British/Saudi geopolitical crimes.

Yemen: Stop the Carnage, Investigate the Crimes

In Yemen today the death and destruction are solely at the hands of Saudi Arabia. The latest UN report (Sept. 5) estimates the civilian death toll at at least 5,500 in the past two-and-a-half years (over 10,000 deaths total); with thousands more injured. Cholera cases have exceeded 600,000, with at least 2,000 deaths, according to the World Health Organization. Water and sanitation services have been devastated. Millions are dislocated. There are at least 19 million people in need of humanitarian aid, and over 7 million in desperate need of food. But the Saudis are blocking relief shipments. The Saudis have bombed multiple hospitals, schools, and social gatherings. Britain and the United States are supplying arms; the United States is providing re-fueling and surveillance.

In releasing details, the UN High Commissioner for Human Rights Zeid Ra'ad al-Hussein said Sept. 5 that Yemenis are suffering from "an entirely manmade catastrophe." On Sept. 11, for the third time in three years, Commissioner Zeid asked the UN Human Rights Council (of 47 nations) to launch an investigation into violations of international humanitarian law.

On Sept. 13 at a Geneva meeting of the Council, China and several other nations indicated their willingness to back such an international inquiry into the atrocities in Yemen. The Chinese delegate said of the idea, that, "We agree with the moves, including the COI [Commission of Inquiry], to promote the political solving of the Yemen crisis." Canada and the Netherlands provided a draft text for the Council to establish a COI. But Britain and the United States opposed it. Saudi Arabia and its cohort nations boycotted the discussion altogether.

Rescue, Rebuild

As horrible as the destruction of life is in Yemen, it is not a "special case." It expresses Anglo-American policy—over the past 60 years—of perpetual war under various banners: regime change, Responsibility to Protect (R2P), human rights, and other pretexts. Look at the series of battleground nations: Afghanistan, Iraq, Libya, Ukraine, and Yemen. Syria has been able to resist, with the assistance of Russia. Before that, Vietnam. This must stop.

We can now break with this horrible legacy and its perpetrators, whose system opposes the general welfare. We can join together in the policy of the New Silk Road, whose capability and intent to serve the common good of mankind, are evident in the way that millions of people in many nations, are collaborating in projects of mutual benefit.

In the United States, there is a new, deep wave of compassion for humanity, and a will for development in the aftermath of the devastation in the Americas from the hurricanes and the Mexican earthquake. Americans are looking forward to the economic projects which must now be done for the future. They are also reflecting on essential projects that were not done—flood defenses, water systems, advanced power infrastructure, space-based climate analysis— because they were claimed to be "too costly," since these crucial infrastructure projects supposedly had to compete with the U.S. commitment to the many wars, from Vietnam, to Afghanistan, to Iraq, and now Yemen.

No more. Never again. We now can rescue and rebuild.

The first version of this statement was issued Sept. 12; it was updated Sept. 16, 2017.

Yemeni Foreign Minister Receives LaRouche Movement Statement on Stopping the Saudi War Against Yemen

Sept. 14—Yesterday, the Foreign Minister of Yemen, Engineer Hisham Sharaf, received in his office in Sana'a the LaRouche Movement statement entitled "Enemy of Silk Road Paradigm: Saudi Genocide in Yemen." It was delivered by Schiller Institute friend Fouad Al-Ghaffari, Chairman of the Yemeni Advisory Office for Coordination with the BRICS, and also the President of the Yemeni Youth Cabinet.

The Yemeni daily *Sana'a News* covered the meeting with a report entitled "The Foreign Minister Receives the Statement of the LaRouche Movement Concerning Yemen and Calling for Stopping the Aggression." The article reported that Al-Ghaffari briefed the minister on the latest international developments concerning Yemen, especially since the Xiamen BRICS Summit, which referenced the situation in Yemen for the first time in its final declaration.

According to *Sana'a News*, Al-Ghaffari "briefed the Foreign Minister on the vision adopted by Mrs. Helga Zepp-LaRouche, who is also known as the New Silk Road Lady, calling for an immediate end to the Saudi aggression on Yemen, and who calls for including Yemen in the New Silk Road initiative." *Sana'a News* reports that the LaRouche Movement statement calls for establishing an international commission to investigate the crimes committed by the Saudi regime, which is known for its aggressive character since its creation, and which is now targeting the program of President Trump.

Al-Ghaffari also briefed the Minister on the efforts being made in the U.S. Congress to stop the sales of arms and ammunition to Saudi Arabia, and that activists in Washington are pushing Congress to end support for the Saudi war that has claimed the lives of at least 10,000 Yemeni civilians and has blocked delivery of food and medicines to millions, causing the greatest humanitarian catastrophe in the country.

Sana'a News also reported that the members of the LaRouche Movement are planning to distribute their statement at the UN General Assembly building in New York, as well as at the conference of the United Nations High Commission for Human Rights in Geneva. It further adds that the statement stresses that the aggression against Yemen is part of the regime-change policies that have been pursued by the United States and Britain for decades, and that this barbarism can only be outflanked by the rallying around the New Silk Road paradigm.

Sana'a News states the following in the conclusion of its report: "It is noteworthy that His Excellency Eng. Hisham Sharaf had expressed in a letter to his Chinese counterpart in April, the desire for Yemen to join the New Silk Road. The Xiamen Declaration of the BRICS nations has now opened a very important window for Yemen that can be utilized to send a message to the Foreign Ministers of the BRICS, who are intending to meet on the sidelines of the 72nd Session of the UN General Assembly, and to bring the situation in Yemen to the UN Security Council."

It is a tragic mistake that the members of the United Nations do not recognize the government in Sana'a as the representative of the Yemeni people and their interests—rather they recognize the five-star-hotel resident in Riyadh, Saudi Arabia, Abed Rabbo Mansour Hadi and his entourage as the legitimate government of Yemen. Hadi's mandate as acting president had expired before the Ansarullah (Houthis) put him under house arrest in late 2014. He is being used by the Saudis as a tool to continue the destruction of Yemen, as he has refused to hold any negotiations with the popularly-approved government in Sana'a, composed of members of Ansarullah and the National Congress Party of former President Ali Abdullah Saleh. Foreign Minister Sharaf is a member of the latter party.

For more information about Al-Ghaffari, visit his Facebook page: https://www.facebook.com/FouadAl-ghaffari

IV. The Great Projects of the LaRouches

China's Maritime Silk Road Puts Kra Canal Back on the Global Agenda

by Mike Billington

Sept. 18—The potential for the building of a canal across the Kra Isthmus in southern Thailand (called either the Kra Canal or the Thai Canal) has taken a huge step forward as a result of a highly successful conference in Bangkok on Sept. 11, titled: "Technology for Sustainable Paths to Thailand's Future— Thai Canal: Comprehensive Study of Alternative Logistics Systems for the Maritime Silk Road."

This is the culmination of over 35 years of organizing, involving scientific and political institutions, primarily led by Pakdee Tanapura, the current head of the Kra Canal Study Team, within Thailand, and by the LaRouche-affiliated political movements around the world. The conference demonstrated significant support for the project from within Thailand (although the government has not as yet officially adopted it) and from nations across Eurasia.

The major difference today, relative to any time over past decades, is the emergence of the the One Belt One Road (OBOR) Initiative under Chinese leadership, which is bringing together dozens of nations from nearly every part of the world, in a joint effort to create a new paradigm for the future of Mankind based on cooperation in building large-scale infrastructure projects to facilitate agro-industrial development. Prof. Zhou Dawei from Peking University, one of the speakers at the conference, told the audi-

EIRNS

Gen. Saiyud Kerdphol, former Supreme Commander of the Thai Armed Forces, addressing the 1984 EIR Bangkok conference. From the left, Pakdee Tanapura; Dr. Zainuddin Bahari of Malaysia's Institute for Strategic and Economic Studies; Dr. Norio Yamamoto of Japan; and Dr. Svasti Srisukh, former Thai secretary general of the Office of Atomic Energy for Peace. On the right, K.L. Dalal, former Indian Ambassador to Thailand; and Dr. H. Roesian Abdulgam, advisor to Indonesian President Suharto.

ence: "We strongly believe that under the OBOR initiative, if we give more importance to the Kra Isthmus Canal project, we will definitely be part of a great change in humankind's history."

EIRNS

Lyndon LaRouche speaking at the Development of the Pacific and Indian Oceans Basin conference in Bangkok, Thailand, Oct. 27, 1983. Pakdee Tanapura is on the right.

The idea for such a canal has been imagined since the 18th Century. More recently, the idea was brought forward as one of the "Great Projects" proposed by Lyndon LaRouche and his Fusion Energy Foundation in the early 1980s, in collaboration with Masaki Nakajima, the visionary head of the Mitsubishi Global Infrastructure Fund (GIF) in Japan. In addition to the Kra Canal, the proposed projects included:
• The greening of the African and Arab deserts

- The transfer of water from the Congo River to replenish Lake Chad in Central Africa
- A bridge over the Bering Strait
- Creating a lake in the Qattara Depression in Egypt
- A New Silk Road from China through Central Asia to Europe and Africa.

All of these projects, and many more, are now being implemented, in one stage or another, under the concept of the OBOR, the New Silk Road.

Working with the Thai government, the LaRouche organization and the GIF co-sponsored two conferences in Bangkok in 1983 and 1984, called, respectively, "The Development of the Pacific and Indian Ocean Basins," and "The Kra Canal and the Industrialization of Thailand."

Drawing on a feasibility study published in 1973 by the TAMS engineering firm and the Lawrence Livermore National Laboratories in the United States, the 1983 and 1984 conferences featured LaRouche, Pakdee Tanapura, representatives of TAMS, Lawrence Livermore, and the GIF, and representatives from many of the nations in the region.

In his presentations there, Lyndon LaRouche's focus was that the Kra Canal was not needed just to expedite shipping, but that southern Thailand must function as a hub for the rapid development of the Indian-Pacific Oceans region, recognizing that Asia would rapidly become the productive motor for reversing the decline of the world economy following the assassination of John Kennedy, and the United States being drawn into colonial warfare in Indochina, on behalf of the British empire.

Among the prominent Thai speakers was Gen. Saiyud Kerdphol, the former Supreme Commander, who noted that: "We must recognize that economic, political and social development all contribute to security, but that security, in itself, is not development."

Gen. Saiyud is still today an active promoter of the Kra Canal, and sent a long message to this month's conference, in which he called for the building of the Canal to be declared a "Royal Project," in order to circumvent political and related obstruction.

Unlike in the 1980s, the new King of Thailand, Maha Vajiralongkorn, is said to support the Kra Canal project, and several leaders of the Privy Council, including its current President (and a former Prime Minister) Prem Tinsulanonda, are strong supporters. The new King will

thai canal news

International conference on the Thai (Kra) Canal, Bangkok, Sept. 11.

soon be officially crowned, after the cremation ceremony for his father King Bhumibol in October.

Such Royal support could well be enough to convince Prime Minister Prayut Chan-ocha to endorse the project. Prayut's military regime has thus far successfully prevented any recurrence of the chaos and near civil war that existed before his takeover in 2014, but he has maintained that the Kra Canal would have to wait for the next administration, to be elected some time in the next few years. Prayut has, however, worked closely with China and was one of the five leaders invited to China for the BRICS Summit earlier this month, as part of what Xi Jinping called the "BRICS Plus." On the sidelines of that event, the final agreement for China to build the first high speed railroad in Thailand was signed, and is to begin construction in October.

The Conference

Japan's *Nikkei Asian Review* reported on the conference on Sept. 11, under the title: "European Business Joins in Pushing $28 bn Thai Canal" and led with the speech of Rolf-Dieter Daniel, president of the European Association for Business and Commerce, the umbrella group of European chambers of commerce in Thailand. Daniel told the conference: "We believe the project should have a very high priority for the government," and, if approved, would be one of the most ambitious and transformational infrastructure projects ever contemplated in Asia. "As the canal offers tremendous advantages for freight traffic between Eastern Asia, Japan, and China and the West, India and Europe, we are sure that international shipping is willing to pay appropriate charges."

Peking University's Prof. Zhou Dawei, quoted above, also said that the Thai Canal "would make Thai-

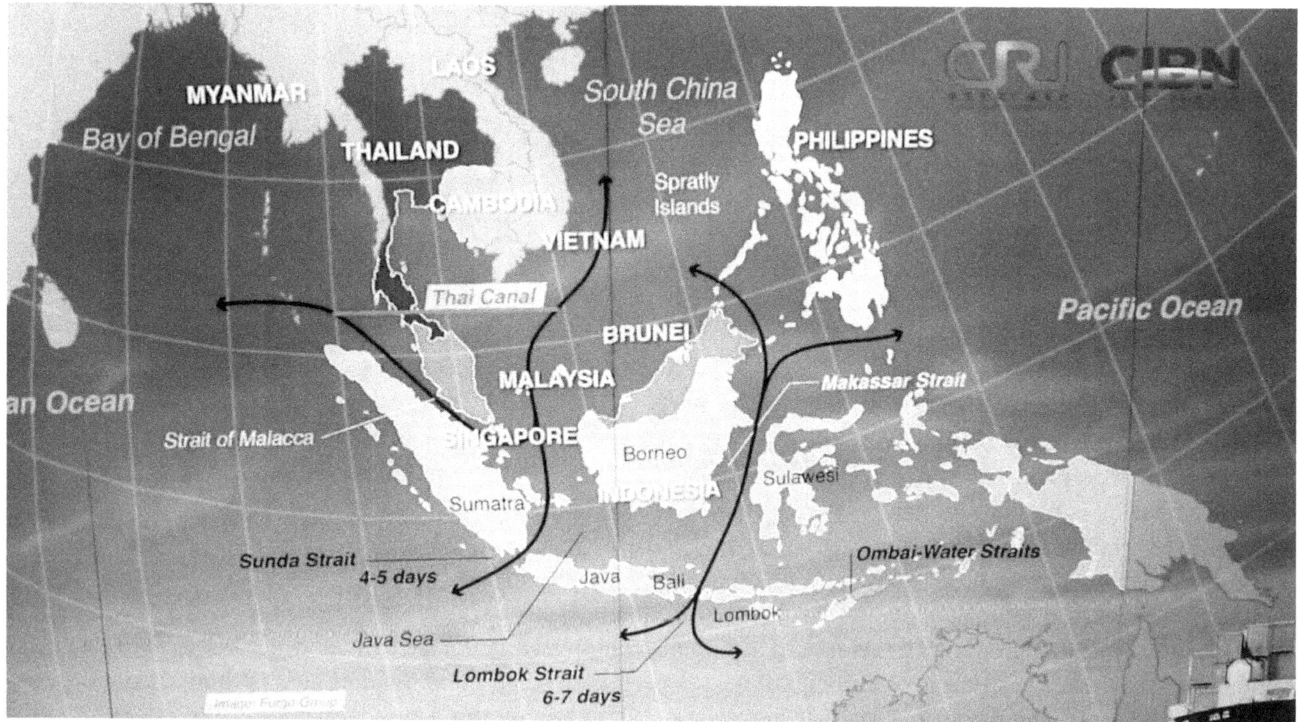

thai canal news

Strategic location of the proposed Thai Canal.

land a true transport hub in the world," and that it contributed to the One Belt One Road "in reviving the famous ancient trade routes that link Asia, Africa, and Europe," according to the Malaysian news agency Bernama. Zhou compared the Kra Canal with global mega-projects such as the Three Gorges Dam in China and the Channel Tunnel linking Britain and France. "If we are lucky enough, we expect that in the near future, the Thai Canal will also appear on this amazing list," he said.

Also attending the conference were 30 residents of the southern Thai region where the Canal will be built. They were there to refute those who claim the local community would oppose the mega-project. Gen. Pongthep Tesprateep, the Chairman of the Thai Canal Association, told the *Bangkok Post* that they had already gathered over 200,000 signatures in support from academics, associations, and citizens in the region along the proposed Canal route. Pakdee Tanapura noted that ports and industrial parks to be built on either end of the Canal will provide a huge number of jobs for local residents, in an area which has been plagued by Muslim-Buddhist conflicts and terrorist activity for many years. Social instability is not a reason to question the project, just the opposite—it is the necessary basis to build peace through opportunity and development.

Chuan Phukaoluan, chief adviser to the governor of Krabi (a province on the Indian Ocean side of the Kra Isthmus) said the Canal will trigger a demand for and expansion of higher education in engineering and vocational training in the region: "This could lift the level of education and the skill of laborers in the South."

Great Projects Under Way

The explosive process of development generated by the New Silk Road in the former colonial nations in Asia, Africa, the Middle East, and Ibero-America, is breathtaking, after several centuries of colonial and post-colonial rule in which the western powers declared to these nations that big infrastructure projects and modern industry were not "appropriate" to their level of development.

Now we see railroads being built across Africa and Asia, not only to get the raw materials from the mines to the ports for export, but railroads connecting the continent's major cities and capitals. Discussions are underway for a transoceanic railroad in South America. Massive water diversion is taking place in China, in Africa, and potentially in the Middle East, to end droughts and floods, creating new agricultural lands and the basis for new cities. Nuclear power plants are being built in nations for the first time.

These are the projects carefully developed by institutions under Lyndon LaRouche's direction over the past

45 years. Read the review of La-Rouche's programmatic proposals since his 1975 plan for an International Development Bank, including extensive development proposals for India, Africa, Ibero-America, and the Indian and Pacific Oceans Basin—all pointing to his New Silk Road concept after the fall of the Soviet Union. You can see such a review at: https://larouchepac.com/new-economic-order.

Not only the Kra Canal, but nearly all these projects are now coming to fruition or are in preparation. And yet the United States is playing no part, and receiving no benefit from this world-historic transformation. No representatives of the United States attended the Kra Canal conference this month, despite invitations sent to the U.S. Embassy in Bangkok.

President Trump has made it clear that he recognizes the urgency of America's engagement with the New Silk Road, and of American cooperation with Russia and China in bringing peace through development to the world—including emphatically to the de-caying United States economy. This is the reason for the ongoing coup attempt against him. The more rapidly he and the American people fully adopt and efficiently make known their support for the LaRouche Great Projects approach, the sooner we can end the dark era of perpetual warfare, and realize a new paradigm of peace and development.

Participants at the Sept. 11 conference on the "Thai Canal: Comprehensive Study of Alternative Logistics Systems for the Maritime Silk Road."

The New Silk Road Becomes the World Land-Bridge

The BRICS countries have a strategy to prevent war and economic catastrophe. It's time for the rest of the world to join!

This 374-page report is a road-map to the New World Economic Order that Lyndon and Helga LaRouche have championed for over 20 years.

Includes:

Introduction by Helga Zepp-LaRouche, "The New Silk Road Leads to the Future of Mankind!"

The metrics of progress, with emphasis on the scientific principles required for survival of mankind: nuclear power and desalination; the fusion power economy; solving the water crisis.

The three keystone nations: China, the core nation of the New Silk Road; Russia's mission in North Central Eurasia and the Arctic; India prepares to take on its legacy of leadership.

Other regions: The potential contributions of Southwest, Central, and Southeast Asia, Australia, Europe, and Africa.

The report is available in PDF $35
and in hard copy $50 (softcover) $75 (hardcover)
plus shipping and handling.

Order from http://store.larouchepub.com

Dialogue Among Cultures: The Road to Peace

by Lyndon H. LaRouche, Jr.

People have too often excused their lack of initiative to change existing policies, by arguing that history often appears to repeat itself. In fact, in nearly every crisis, mankind has always had within it the potential, and the moral responsibility, to change the course of history for the betterment of the human condition. So it is at the present moment of grave international financial and other crises. Now, once again, we again face the challenge of changing our fate, by an appropriate act of the human will. Today, the nations still have time to choose, during a relatively short period of time now before us, not to repeat the presently looming threat of religious wars and dark ages which have spoiled the progress of mankind most greatly during past cycles of both medieval and modern history.

On this occasion, I have three leading points to submit. First, I wish to define the meaning of a dialogue among cultures, in a way which is perhaps unique, but I think necessary, among the proposals I have heard made on this subject, from around the world, so far. Second, I wish to emphasize the role of economic policy in defining the crucial, practical objectives of such a dialogue. Third, I wish to make clear the way in which certain powerful Anglo-American interests, such as Zbigniew Brzezinski's Samuel P. Huntington, and others, intend to foment religious warfare, as a way of preventing a dialogue among cultures from occurring. I shall begin by focussing upon the continuing part played by the willful instigation of religious warfare in modern European history.

1. Religious Warfare in Modern History

To situate the present discussion, consider but a few of those cycles of religious and related forms of warfare, which we should study as lessons from nearby past history, lessons to be applied to that deadly combination of growing potential for such warfare, in a strategic situation, today, which is otherwise defined by a presently onrushing general financial collapse confronting every part of the world. My attention is focussed upon the willful orchestration of religious warfare, when used by great powers as a strategic weapon of conflict.

For example, for nearly a century and a half, from the 1511 victory of Venice over the League of Cambrai, until the 1648 Treaty of Westphalia, Europe was dominated by religious warfare. The Thirty Years War of 1618-1648, which produced the conditions of a new dark age in Central Europe, as during the earlier war of the Hapsburgs against the Netherlands, typified the entire period from about the A.D. 1511 formation of the so-called Holy League, until the 1648 peace of Westphalia.

These religious wars of the 1511-1648 interval, had been organized by the same Venice which had dominated the Mediterranean as an imperial maritime power, since what was called the Fourth Crusade (A.D. 1202-1204), through which Venice conquered and looted Byzantium. It was this same Venice, with its Norman allies, which, earlier, had organized the warfare and

From the 1511 victory of Venice over the League of Cambrai, until the 1648 Treaty of Westphalia, Europe was dominated by religious warfare. Left: The facade of St. Mark's in Venice.

The Thirty Years War produced conditions of a new dark age in Central Europe (below).

other ruin which brought about a great collapse of European civilization during the period from about A.D. 1239 through the so-called New Dark Age of the middle of the following century.

This same Venice continued that role, even after the Westphalia peace, for as long as it continued its position, as a leading, if fading imperial maritime power, until near the close of the Seventeenth Century. In its post-1511 counterattack on the great reforms introduced under the Fifteenth-century Renaissance, Venice had not only orchestrated, but, to a large degree, created these warring religious factions of the 1511-1648 interval, most of which factions consisted of duped fools who were nominally Christian. By means of these Venice-directed religious conflicts, Venice managed to put those emerging sovereign nation-states of Europe, such as France, England, and the German states, which had been allied against Venice prior to A.D. 1511, at one another's throats.

Even during that 1511-1648 interval, there was some continuation of that splendid legacy of progress in art, science, and statecraft, which had been introduced by the Italy-centered, Fifteenth-century Renais-sance. But, nonetheless, Europe as a whole was plunged into what some historians have correctly described as a "little new dark age," only less terrible than the earlier New Dark Age of Europe's Fourteenth Century. It was only through the peace secured by the 1648 Treaty of Westphalia, that a somewhat civilized degree of progress and stability was achieved in Europe. The general progress in European economy and political institutions, continued during the often war-torn two and a half centuries following that 1648 treaty, until a turning-point was reached, as a result of the 1901 assassination of U.S. President William McKinley.

It was that assassination of McKinley, which was conducted in the strategic interest of Britain's King Edward VII, which set into motion an alliance between the British monarchy and its former foe, the United States, which unleashed all of the great wars and related conflicts which dominated most of the Twentieth Century, up to the present time.

It is important to recognize, that the orchestration of military and kindred forms of strategic conflict, during the entirety of the period following World War I, and until the collapse of the Soviet system during 1989-1991, were organized in the form of religious warfare, largely around the theme of that "crusade against communism" of which Hitler's Nazi regime had been a product and part.

Notably, in all three of these cited cases, that leading into the New Dark Age of the Fourteenth Century, the "little new dark age" of 1511-1648, and the great wars of the Anglo-American Twentieth Century, these financier-oligarchical factions which dominate the ruling financier circles of the Anglo-American alliance of today, were always products of a specific imperial factor of influence. Contrary to the generally accepted mythologies, these wars were not rooted in conflicts in national interests of nations as nations, but were essentially ideological conflicts, either as religious wars, or ideological conflicts, such as the anti-communist crusades, which were of the same character as religious wars.

During the Thirteenth through Seventeenth Centuries, for example, Venice, as an imperial maritime and financier-oligarchical power, was the determining influence. In every case, the war was either orchestrated by Venice itself, or by a form of financier-oligarchical interest which had been built up according to the Venice model.

In later times, it has been the Anglo-Dutch financial-oligarchical interest, which is the model imitated by the rentier-financier interests of Wall Street today. These Anglo-Dutch interests, as typified by the Dutch and British East India Companies, were created, during the course of the Sixteenth and Seventeenth Centuries by Venice's powerful financier oligarchy, and modelled themselves, as merchant-banking maritime powers, upon the Venice which had, in fact, authored what became the Dutch and British financier oligarchy of the Seventeenth and Eighteenth cenTuries. Indeed, since the last decades of the Sixteenth Century and early decades of the Seventeenth, it was Paolo Sarpi, then the lord of Venice, who created that empiricist ideology of Thomas Hobbes, John Locke, Bernard Mandeville, and Adam Smith, the ideology which, as Henry Kissinger emphasized in his May 10, 1982 Chatham House keynote, is the empiricist way of thinking which shapes the characteristic mind-set and global behavior of the Anglo-American financier oligarchy, and Kissinger himself, still today.

Still, today, the same legacies of religious warfare from the past are actively promoted, as so-called geopolitical conflicts against China and others, by the financier-oligarchy's New York Council on Foreign Relations.

Today, the same use of orchestrated religious warfare, as organized by Venice over the interval from the Fourth Crusade through 1648, has been unleashed again, in the aftermath of the 1989-1991 collapse of the Soviet system. The world as a whole is now hovering at the brink of a threatened, planet-wide new dark age. The outbreak of religious warfare, under these circumstances of global economic crisis, could ensure that the threatened dark age becomes a reality.

Since the Fifteenth-century introduction of a new form of society, the modern form of sovereign nation-state, and, especially since the 1648 Treaty of Westphalia, the old cyclical pattern has taken on a significantly modified form. In this form, it is the cycles of recurring economic crisis which supply a critical element of impulse and timing, for the modern cycles of religious warfare and kindred conflicts.

Look at the present threat of such religious warfare, and of related kinds of ideological warfare, from the standpoint of what the world as a whole should have learned from Europe's experience of 1511-1648. Let us examine this history with that patient consideration implied in the famous remarks of one notable Harvard Professor Santayana, that those who fail to learn from the history I have just referenced, are therefore condemned to repeat it.

2. The Global Strategic Crisis of Today

To understand the specific qualities of the past decade of unfolding world history, we must focus on axiomatic changes in the correlation of political and economic power which developed during and since the 1989-1991 collapse of the Soviet Union as a leading strategic force.

Beginning 1990, the forces represented by Britain's Prime Minister Margaret Thatcher, France's President François Mitterrand, and the U.S.A.'s President George Bush, Sr., orchestrated an armed conflict between Iraq and Kuwait, which was then used, as a pretext, for unleashing a war against Iraq, which has, in fact, been continued up to the present moment.

Left to right: Zbigniew Brzezinski, Samuel Huntington, and Henry Kissinger, theoreticians of the "Clash of Civilizations."

The launching of this London-directed war against Iraq, was immediately followed by the unleashing of a series of new Balkan wars, launched under the direction of those British and French interests which had controlled Balkan politics since the post-Versailles Trianon treaty. That Balkan war has been continued, like the Thirty Years War of 1616-1648, and also the Balkan wars preceding World War I, in an evolving form, up to the present moment.

During the same recent period, through the present moment, there has been an orchestrated effort to drown much of Europe in what Zbigniew Brzezinski's associate, Professor Samuel P. Huntington, has proposed should be fostered to become a "Clash of Civilizations," a term which, the Professor has indicated, signifies the intent to manage the politics of nations throughout our planet, by provoking a great conflagration, in the general form of religious warfare, pivotted upon the inciting of a more or less interminable and bloody conflict between Islam and the West.

Professor Huntington's and his associates' proposal, for a nearly planet-wide religious conflict of European civilization against the Islamic world, has been intended as a detonator for this new wave of religious warfare, and has been the setting into motion of the al-ready existing explosive charge of three generations of bloody Arab-Israeli conflict.

At this moment, the intent is to deploy the lunatic types of U.S. Protestant fundamentalists, such as President-elect George Bush's nominee John Ashcroft, closely associated with the incoming U.S. Bush Administration, to foster an atrocity against the sacred Dome of the Rock in Jerusalem, for the purpose of detonating the potential for a new Israeli-Arab war. This war is intended, not only to continue the destruction of Arab states such as Syria and Iraq, but to engage Iran, too, as a target of Israeli attacks, and thus spread the warfare through regions of the world associated with Muslim populations and their neighbors.

We see the same thrust expressed in the fomenting of religious and related strife, organized by the former Anglo-Dutch and Portuguese colonial powers, within Indonesia, and in the hateful targetting of Malaysia by such persons as U.S. Vice-President Al Gore and Gore's accomplice, the avowedly fanatical follower of H.G. Wells, Secretary of State Madeleine Albright. We see the intent of certain Anglo-American interests, to ignite new waves of communalist warfare in the sub-continent of Asia.

Like the religious wars orchestrated by the imperial

maritime power of Venice, during the 1511-1648 interval, the threat of widespread religious warfare today, also has a readily defined architecture, as this is merely typified by the close personal, extended family relationship, across Party lines, of Samuel P. Huntington associate Zbigniew Brzezinski to Mrs. Albright, her father Josef Korbel, and Korbel's protégé, U.S. President-elect Bush's advisor, Condoleezza Rice.

Ironically, but not accidentally, the motives for Venice's orchestration of the 1511-1648 religious warfare, and the motives of Brzezinski, Huntington, and others, for seeking to unleash a so-called "Clash of Civilizations" today, are essentially the same.

Then, in 1511-1648, Venice's motive was to destroy that process of establishing modern forms of sovereign nation-states, such as those which had been founded by France's Louis XI and England's Henry VII. In this, the Venice-directed Holy League and its sequels nearly succeeded. It was the Treaty of Westphalia, which rescued the modern form of sovereign nation-state from the same fate as Europe of the Fourteenth-century New Dark Age. It was the establishment of international law by the Treaty of Westphalia, which permitted the institution of the modern nation-state to emerge as the characteristic institution of modern European civilization.

Today, the form of that conflict is somewhat different; many of the names have changed; but the pattern is essentially the same. Today, the orchestrated ideological form of global conflict, is a conflict with the imperial interest of the Five English-Speaking Powers, an interest stated in such purely ideological language as "globalization" and "rule of law," symbolic terms which express a revival of the notions of empire and law associated with pagan Rome, terms which express a religious quality of hateful opposition to the principle of the sovereign nation-state.

The ruin of Soviet power, during 1989-1991, encouraged the powers associated then with Britain's Prime Minister Margaret Thatcher, France's President François Mitterrand, and the U.S.A.'s President George Bush, to declare those five English-speaking powers, the Queen of England's United Kingdom, Canada, Australia, and New Zealand, and the U.S.A., as an Anglo-American world-government in fact and force.

Thus, under the latter reign of the 1989-2000 period, not only have measures been taken to destroy the legal basis for the sovereign form of nation-state, but the economic basis as well. Policies of "free trade" and "globalization," combined with the curious use of the name of "democracy" by Brzezinski's Huntington, represent the effort to establish a style of world-wide imperial rule modelled not only upon the "geopolitical maritime" model of medieval and modern Venice, but also upon the precedent of ancient pagan Rome, a neo-Roman form of imperialism based upon what some have called, euphemistically, "the rule of law," more honestly described as "the imperial rule of Roman law."

The Anglo-American impulse behind this development of 1989-1991, did not begin at the close of the 1980s; exactly such goals had been the goal of the British monarchy since the 1901 assassination of U.S. President McKinley, an assassination which brought financier interests associated with the former slave-holding Confederacy and Wall Street finance into a close alliance with imperial Britain. This was, for example, the repeatedly declared intent of the principal author of the nuclear bombing of Hiroshima and Nagasaki, Bertrand Russell, the intent to compel nations to dissolve their sovereignties in favor of a Roman-style, imperial form of world government.

The connection to 1511-1648, goes even deeper than such leading particular sets of facts of modern European history. Imperial Venice was a form of power based upon a financier oligarchy which spread its tentacles throughout the trade, finance, and politics of all Europe. The Anglo-American interest represented by the would-be imperial Thatcher-Mitterrand-Bush cabal of 1989-1991, and by the matching U.S. Thornburgh doctrine, represents the same kind of special oligarchical interest.

Thus, today, once again, the peace and stability of our planet is threatened, by the unleashing of those kinds of orchestrated religious warfare, which are the most difficult kinds of war to bring to an end, and the most likely to bring a new dark age upon either some large area of our planet, or, even, the planet as a whole. So, it is urgent that we, today, learn certain valuable lessons from the recent eight centuries of today's now globally extended European civilization; it is important to recognize points of historical coincidence between what was achieved by the 1648 Treaty of Westphalia, and what has been lately proposed, as by such leading figures as the President of Iran, as a dialogue among cultures.

3. The Economics of a doomed System

Although the use of religious warfare as a strategic weapon is very ancient, the Twentieth-century cycle has crucial features which make the present world economic crisis qualitatively different than any other crisis of the preceding two centuries of the history of today's globally extended form of modern European culture.

During the Twentieth Century, until about 1966-1971, the overall trend in economic development was for an increase in the average productive powers of labor, and for improvements in demographic characteristics of the population of Europe and the Americas, in particular. Beginning about thirty-five years ago, beginning during the 1966-1968 Presidential campaign of Richard Nixon, there was an orchestrated resurgence, within my U.S.A., of the pro-racist forms of allied, so-called "Christian fundamentalist" and what Israel's David Ben-Gurion had once condemned as pro-fascist, "right-wing Zionist" beliefs, which, taken together, are the chief mass-based expressions of ideological impulses behind the Southern Strategy factions in the Republican Party, as introduced under President Jimmy Carter, to the Democratic Party, too. Under the influence of this ideological influence on U.S. policy-shaping, the demographic characteristics of the Americas and Europe have been moving, by intention, along a downward course.

Typical of this downward trend, has been the spread and intensification of pro-Malthusian policies, and the systemic destruction of the economies of those and other regions of the world under those influences. Once the Soviet system ceased to be a strategic rival of the trans-Atlantic power, the governments of those powers moved, immediately, to bring about a general destruction of those institutions of basic-economic infrastructure, agriculture, and industry, upon which the strength and security of nations had depended up to that time. This savage destruction of the former "full-set economic potentials" of national economies, unleashed with full force, globally, during the recent decade, represents an acceleration of economically suicidal trends in the same direction launched within the U.S.A., and elsewhere, in the aftermath of both the assassination of U.S. President John F. Kennedy, and President Lyndon Johnson's sponsorship of two civil-rights laws whose enactment enraged the traditional racist currents within the U.S.A.

This coincidence between the rise of pro-racist policies in the leadership of both the Republican and Democratic parties of the U.S.A., and the promotion of so-called neo-Malthusian, and also racialist policies for economy and population-control, was never accidental. This connection is best understood from inspection of the relevant internal history of the U.S. itself. This connection exposes the crucial problem which must be overcome, if we are to enjoy the cooperation and other benefits to be sought through a dialogue among cultures.

The institution of chattel slavery, as practiced in the U.S.A. upon persons designated as of African descent, is much more than an obvious crime against the victims of such inhumanity. Such practice of slavery, as upheld by the authors of the treasonous conspiracy known as the Confederate States of America, expresses a conception of mankind which is intrinsically contrary to the conception of man under the Mosaic doctrine common to Christianity, and Islam. The forces which have seized a dominant position in the political parties of the U.S.A. since Nixon's 1966 launching of the Republican Party's Southern Strategy, are premised upon the Confederacy's perverted and degenerate conception of the nature of man. Many of the supporters of that neo-Confederate political outlook, such as the popular base of the Bush Republicans such as President-elect Bush's nominee John Ashcroft, and the Gore Democrats, profess themselves to be Christians; obviously, they are not.

Not only are such neo-Confederate cultural outlooks intrinsically racist, and therefore anti-Christian and anti-Islam. The political and economic policies of those pro-racist currents are fully congruent with their pro-bestial, virtually satanic misconception of the nature and rights of the human individual personality.

On this account, the issues of economy and dialogue of cultures, become immediately one and the same.

The modern form of European civilization, the form known as the sovereign nation-state republic, derived its conception of economy and politics from a long struggle in Europe to establish forms of nation and economy which are consistent with Christian civilization's conception of the essential nature of man, as a creature made in the image of the Creator.

Thus, the revolutionary, modern form of European sovereign nation-state, as first defined during the Fifteenth-century Renaissance, was premised on the notion that government has no moral authority under law, except as that government is efficiently committed to the promotion of the general welfare of both all of the living and their posterity. In other words, earlier forms of society, in which some men treated the majority of humanity as virtually human cattle, were to be outlawed. Society must be constituted, as obliged by its highest law, natural law, to express and protect that quality of the individual person which coheres with the notion of man as made in the image of the Creator.

Thus, the modern sovereign form of nation-state, as expressed by the U.S. 1776 Declaration of Independence, like the policies which informed Louis XI's France and Henry VII's England during the late Fifteenth Century, emphasizes the fostering of those creative powers of scientific and other discovery, by means of which each person may be enabled to participate in and contribute to the progress of the human condition from one generation to the next. As this policy was set forth by Nicholas of Cusa, during the Fifteenth Century, this requires that we adopt as an objective an ecumenical fraternity among sovereign nations, such that each is pledged to promote the common good for its own people, and to cooperate in a community of principle among nations, to promote the common good of them all.

In contrast to this, today's U.S. ideological followers of the Confederacy's tradition, insist on placing the "free trade" interest, and that of so-called "shareholder value," not only above human values, but even as opposed to human values. They not only oppose, but denounce that principled dedication to the general welfare, which is the highest constitutional law of the U.S. republic.

In the history of progress within modern European civilization, the building-up of the means for scientific and technological gains in the productive powers, and conditions of life, of labor in general, was expressed in large-scale promotion of basic economic infrastructure, chiefly by government, and the fostering of credit to assist farmers, industrial entrepreneurs, and others, in prospering in those activities which represented a contribution to progress in the general welfare of the society as a whole.

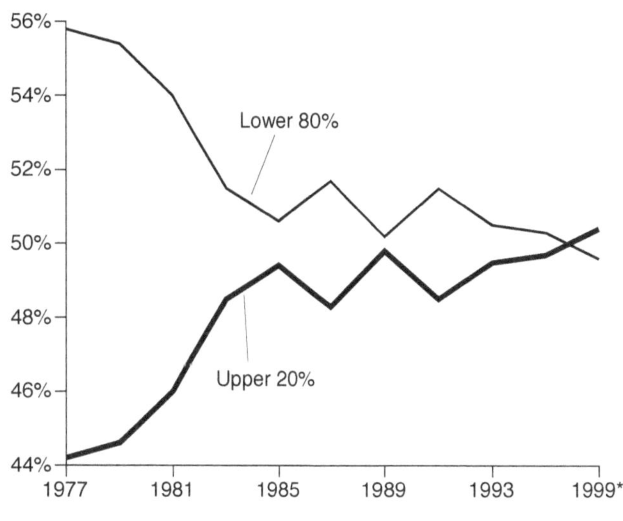

FIGURE 1

Since Jimmy Carter: America's Richest 20% Now Make More than the Other 80%

(percent of total U.S. personal income)

*Projected
Sources: Congressional Budget Office; *EIR*.

The economic forces associated with such progress, include progressive individual farmers, entrepreneurs, technologically progressive forces of industrial labor, and the scientific and other professions essential to fostering such progress.

The 1966-2000 attempt of the neo-Confederacy forces to re-establish and consolidate the traditions of the slaveholders' Confederacy, has been expressed in a rabid effort to eliminate the political power of those combined, agricultural, industrial, and professional forces in society, on which support for the principle of the general welfare depended. Thus, the lower eighty percent of the family-income brackets of the U.S.A., which commanded the overwhelming majority of the total national income in 1977, when Jimmy Carter become President, have been reduced, by Carter's and other policies, to far less than half the total today [see **Figure 1**].

Thus, in the U.S.A., Europe, and elsewhere, since the mid-1960s, we have witnessed a malicious and increasingly savage commitment to the destruction of those elements of infrastructure, agriculture, industry, and relevant learned professions, on which the successes of pre-1966 economy depended, in the U.S.A., Europe, and elsewhere.

Because of the extensive destruction of those elements of national and world economy, on which the pre-1966 recovery of the U.S. and European economies depended absolutely, we have reached the year 2001 in a global condition far worse than that of the 1929-1931 financial collapse. The successes of the neo-Confederacy and like-minded forces of neo-Malthusianism, globalization, and related utopianism, have destroyed the sub-structure of the world's economy to such a degree, that the economic crisis now gripping the world, is no mere business-cycle or similar crisis; this planet, for the first in modern history, now faces a general economic-breakdown crisis.

This consideration points out the crucial role a dialogue among cultures must play in preventing the plunge of the entire planet into a global form of new dark age for all humanity.

4. Economics, Politics, and Faith

The possibility of avoiding such a new dark age, requires a great degree of emphasis upon the economic side of the discussion. Economics, if properly defined, as physical economy, rather than price-accounting, was created as an expression of that conception of the nature of man as a creature made in the image of God, to exert dominion over all other things. This notion of physical economy, provides the foundation upon which various cultures' agreement in practice must be premised.

Economics as a scientific practice of statecraft, was first developed during Europe's Fifteenth Century. This occurred as a by-product of a then new, revolutionary design in statecraft, a design upon which the continuation of the institution of the modern form of sovereign nation-state depends absolutely.

Before that Fifteenth-century reform, the population existed for the pleasure, comfort, and power of a ruling oligarchy and its lackeys. This was the kind of oligarchical society defended by the reactionary Dr. Quesnay's doctrine of laissez-faire. It was the introduction of the principle, that the moral legitimacy of government depends upon its efficient commitment to promote the improvement of the general welfare of the entire population and its posterity, which was the act of birth of political-economy, with the

emergence of such pioneering new forms of government under France's Louis XI and England's Henry VII.

Within that context, the core of the basis for the kind of strategic dialogue of cultures needed today, is therefore to be found in that conception of the nature of the human individual which is common to the Mosaic tradition of Judaism, Christianity, and Islam: the conception that each person is made in the likeness of the Creator, and thus endowed with certain innate powers not to be found among the beasts. This is especially true of Christianity and Islam, which have been both characteristically missionary cultures, reaching out to all mankind with this common message, that the individual person is made in the image of the Creator and endowed with powers like those flowing from the Creator Himself.

In particular, for the case of today's globally extended modern European civilization, all of the notable successes, which had been more or less peculiar to the rise of modern European civilization since the Fifteenth-century Renaissance, have been the fruit of basing the notion of modern sovereign form of nation-state upon that conception of the universal nature of the human individual, as a creature made in the image of the Creator, and having the obligations and rights of one bearing that nature.

Thus, this notion of the nature of man is historically characteristic of the modern development of Europe, the Americas, Africa, and the Islamic world generally. In some influential cultures from other parts of the world, this notion of man is not accepted axiomatically, even though there may be sympathy for it, in practice if not necessarily in traditional beliefs.

In those broad terms, such are the conditions of belief around which an efficient form of dialogue of cultures is to be organized. I propose that the following steps are the most essential ones.

First, those of us, who embrace the notion of the nature of the individual person as made, from inception, in the likeness of the Creator of the universe, must establish an ecumenical fraternity among ourselves on the premise of this specific conception of the nature of the person. Through our unanimity on this strictly defined, limited point of ecumenical agreement, we must reach out in dialogue with others, to win them to understanding of certain notions of what may be called "natural law," upon

The basis for the dialogue of cultures needed today, is to be found in the conception that each person is made in the likeness of the Creator. Here, a Polish metal trades instructor trains Kenyans in Nairobi.

which all nations and peoples might premise a suitable fraternity.

Second, we must persuade those who may require such persuasion, that it ought to be the common principle, both within states, and among the members of a community of nations, that government has no legitimate moral authority under rule of natural law, except as it is efficiently committed to promote the general welfare of the entire population and its posterity. This definition of general welfare, sometimes called the common good, must be in accord with the given nature of the human individuality.

Third, from this conception of the common good, we must derive a self-governing sense of mission. It is not sufficient to agree to words on paper. Intention must be expressed in positive action; intention is no more sincere than the commitment to a sense of mission which makes professed intentions real ones. There are grave injustices rampant in the world today, not only those injustices imposed by willful cruelties, but injustices which are the fruit of negligence.

On this third account, the most crucial moral test by which the good will of any nation is to be assessed, is that nation's view of the generally worsening conditions imposed, or otherwise induced within the con-

tinent of Africa, sub-Saharan Africa most emphatically.

It is notable, that U.S. President Franklin Roosevelt, confronted Britain's Prime Minister Winston Churchill on this matter of Africa, during their celebrated wartime confrontation at Casablanca. Roosevelt presented there a rather detailed picture of the large-scale infrastructure-building and related measures to be taken with U.S. support during the post-war period. Roosevelt also warned Churchill that, at the close of the war, the power of the U.S.A. would bring to an end the relics of the colonial and imperial rule by Portuguese, Dutch, British, and French interests, over colonized and semi-colonized parts of the world. Unfortunately, as soon as Roosevelt's premature death had occurred, his successors in power took the side of Churchill against Roosevelt's intentions.

Now, the preceding background so outlined, I come to the meat of the matter.

I propose, that all of the essential features of a relevant form of policy-discussion among cultures can be derived from examining what ought to be considered the shared ecumenical principles among Christianity, Islam, and the Mosaic principle, that all men and women are made equally in the image of the Creator, and endowed with those powers by means of which mankind should exert dominion over other forms of life and non-life alike. When I use the term "natural law," I mean that, as it is also incorporated in the 1776 U.S. Declaration of Independence. If we accept this definition of the individual person's nature as the basis for the universal natural law, by which mankind must govern itself, all of the essential axioms of cooperation among those cultures are implicitly provided.

In that case, if we, sharing such ecumenical commonality, agree, then we must also reach out to our brothers and sisters in cultures which do not necessarily adopt the conception of man shared among the heirs of the Mosaic tradition. We must establish a form of ecumenical comprehension between ourselves and those brothers and sisters.

In considering such a course of action, we should be forewarned by the lessons of the way in which the enemy has utilized the weapons of religious and kindred warfare repeatedly, in the past. Only, as the 1648 Treaty of Westphalia approximates this lesson for the modern European experience, if we are sufficiently committed to a common principle as the fundamental political interest of each of us, in common, as a mission expressed in practice, will we be able to defeat those forces of evil merely typified by the case of Samuel P. Huntington today.

We must also be advised, that commitment to mere letter of ecumenical agreement, is not sufficient. We must give substance to agreement through forms of common practice, which are coherent with that agreement in principle.

What that sense of mission must be, is shown to us, in the simplest way, by considering the span of development of the newborn individual to the point it has become a matured adult. The lessons of economic history show us, that just as the biological maturation of a newborn person requires a period of development spanning about a quarter of a century, so the practical goals which should unite us must be expressed in terms of the benefits our generation will contribute to the role to be played by the children and adolescents of today. I mean, we must concretize our agreements on grounds of moral principle, in terms of those great works to be undertaken over a period of up to twenty-five years, more or less.

Such works are, typically efforts in building-up the essential basic economic infrastructure, on which the future of productive economy depends. This means large-scale development of systems of transportation, water management and sanitation, and power-generation and distribution. It also means the development of the systems of education, public health, and health-care on which the productivity and longevity of the population depends.

On this account, what we do, or fail to do for Africa as a whole, has a special quality of significance for humanity as a whole. There are, of course, great and urgent large-scale developments of the basic economic infrastructure of Eurasia, as there are similar challenges to be made in the Americas as a whole. However, to leave Africa to its own internal resources, would be a crime which would stain the conscience of the world. What we do for Africa, will be an emblem of our conscience, a mission whose success will attest to the fact that we, of all parts of this planet, have become truly human, at last: truly human in our conception of the universality of human nature.

In conclusion, our goals should be chiefly three.

First, we must define that ecumenical conception of man, avoiding conflict respecting other matters of religious beliefs, man as made in the image of the Creator of the universe, from which all notions of rational law are rightly derived.

Second, we must establish a secular agreement of principle among a newly defined community of perfectly sovereign nation-states.

These two policies must be expressed by a third, a commitment to broadly defined physical-economic and related missions, of not less than a quarter-century's span. These missions are of three general types. The first is typified by those kinds of great infrastructure developments on which depends the ability of peoples to develop their nation's land-areas as a whole. The second, typified by education and public health programs, is the development of the potential productivities that their populations as a whole, requires. The third, is the commitment to selected common goals of fundamental scientific and technological progress, to which all peoples shall have the equal right to access.

Such an understanding of the nature of man, matched by such a commitment to a mission for practice, is the foundation upon which a successful dialogue among cultures depends.

After the Houston Flood, 1,000 Turn Out To Commemorate Kennedy Moon Address

by Kesha Rogers

We choose to go to the moon. We choose to go to the moon in this decade and do the other things, not because they are easy, but because they are hard. . . .

Tuesday, Sept. 12, marked the 55th anniversary of President John F. Kennedy's Moon Speech in Rice Stadium. In celebration of that historic event which inspired so many, nearly 1,000 people piled into the Stude Concert Hall on the Rice University Campus. The event marking this historic date was titled, "Failure Is Not an Option: Embodying the Credo, 'We Do This Not Because It Is Easy but Because It Is Hard.'" The featured guest speaker was Apollo 13 Astronaut Fred Haise. Ellen Ochoa, Director of Johnson Space Center, also spoke during a brief moderated question-and-answer session along with Haise.

The President of Rice University, David Leebron, in his opening remarks, quoted these very words uttered by President John F. Kennedy in his first lecture at Rice University on Sept. 12, 1962:

We meet at a college noted for knowledge, in a city noted for progress, in a state noted for strength, and we stand in need of all three, for we meet in an hour of change and challenge, in a decade of hope and fear, in an age of both knowledge and ignorance. The greater our knowledge increases, the greater our ignorance unfolds.

Mr. Leebron explained that in the aftermath of Hurricane Harvey that had devastated the Texas region—as now Irma has done to the Florida coast—those words of John F. Kennedy were just as relevant today as they were when they were first heard 55 years ago.

Eighty-four-year-old astronaut Fred Haise gave an awe-inspiring speech to the packed crowd, which had exceeded everyone's expectations for attendance. He spoke about the history of the United States' manned space program, and the harrowing story of the Apollo 13 mission of 1970. Col. Haise was the Lunar Module pilot for Apollo 13. The mission of Apollo 13 was to land in the Fra Mauro area of the Moon, but an explosion on board the spacecraft forced the crew to circle the Moon instead, without landing, and the Fra Mauro site was reassigned to Apollo 14.

In speaking about his experience aboard Apollo 13, Haise recounted the tragic loss of life on Apollo 1 in 1967, after a fire broke out in the cockpit as the spacecraft was sitting on the launch pad, killing all three astronauts. The lessons learned from that tragic event, and the commitment made then that "failure is not an option," saved the lives of Haise and his crewmates later, as he explained. The sacrifice of those who had lost their lives before, may just have saved the lives of others after them.

I think that this is a notable lesson for today. Will we learn the lesson of Harvey? Will we build the infrastructure we need to ensure that not another life will be lost due to man-made error and negligence? So much has been lost, so many have sacrificed—how will we right the wrongs and make the new discoveries which will ensure a better future ahead?

I asked Col. Haise about the lessons that might be learned from the space program and Apollo, that would help to guide the nation during this period of crisis in the aftermath of the hurricanes.

He responded by emphasizing the importance of having the right leader, the necessity of teamwork for rebuilding and infrastructure, and the need to put fully adequate financial resources into that rebuilding—which can only come from a Federal mission, of the sort that Kennedy understood was needed to make Apollo a success.

During the question-and-answer session, Ochoa toed the line about NASA's increasingly shifting to reliance on privatized space flight, but Col. Haise bluntly pointed out these private companies only exist because of NASA, and, unlike NASA, if they don't make a profit, they cease to have a mission.

Col. Haise concluded by highlighting the unique quality of human beings to make discoveries, unlike any animal. No pig or dolphin can build a spacecraft, he said, but you can. The audience gave his speech a standing ovation and left the room greatly inspired, with great hope for the future.